Data Governance

For The

Executive

Data Governance

For The

Executive

James C. Orr

Senna Publishing, LLC

DATA GOVERNANCE FOR THE EXECUTIVE

Published by Senna Publishing, L.L.C.
12328 Mount Baldy Drive
Colorado Springs, Colorado 80921

Printed in the United States of America
First printing 2011

Book cover design: Matthew W. Orr

Editing staff: Matthew W. Orr and Kelley Vivian

ISBN-13: 978-0-615-53191-5
ISBN-10: 0-6155-3191-1
Library of Congress control number: 1-665307051

To my lovely wife, Kathy

And our children,

Christopher
Matthew
Lisa

Table of Contents

Preface

I am of the mindset that if executives do not support something it is because they do not understand it or it lacks substantive business value and is not worth pursuing. When it comes to data governance both seem to apply. The industry has done a marginal job of explaining data governance to business leaders and an equally poor job of demonstrating and communicating its business value. Executives and organizations continue to struggle with the definition behind data governance, its scope, and the benefit behind it. As a result, too few data governance programs get started let alone fulfill their expectations because upper management and the business do not understand the potential and holistic value this discipline delivers.

Naysayers may argue that the business value simply does not justify the means. For others, including this author, the value of data governance is substantial and reaches far beyond what the industry itself has been able to understand and articulate thus far. The sheer complexity, dynamics, and evolution of data governance reveal a number of reasons why the industry has fallen short in explaining its value to executives. This book is intended to bring clarity to the discipline and close the gap between what the data management industry knows and what executives need to know.

Before we dive into what I hope will be a thought provoking experience, I have to come clean. I know this may sound hypocritical but I despise the term 'data governance'. Yes, I realize it is an industry-endorsed buzz term but I challenge whether the expression has become outdated. I will share my view on this topic in Chapter 1 but it is important to note that I use the terms enterprise information asset management, information asset management, and data governance interchangeably throughout this book.

I also use the word 'data' rather liberally throughout this manuscript. Unless otherwise noted I am actually making a blanket reference to any information pertaining but not limited to:

- Customers
- Prospects
- Patients
- Citizens
- Applicants

- Members
- Guests
- Employees
- Partners
- Suppliers

- Agencies
- Products
- Parts
- Services
- Finances
- Content

- Assets
- Policies
- Contracts
- Events
- Transactions
- Parishioners

In most cases, but not always, it is more about reference data rather than financial transaction data.

Structured and unstructured data also is included in my loose definition of data. While most data governance initiatives deal with structured data within databases it is important to note the value of unstructured data (policy, contracts, E-mail, video, spreadsheets, documents, etc.) and the role data governance can play in securing, managing, and bringing together both data types at the right time and for the right reasons.

The concepts expressed here apply to nearly every company, business, agency, or institution that has sizeable operations and data challenges, regardless of industry. For example, nearly every mid-market to large enterprise corporation falls into this category, as do a number of federal, state, regional, and local agencies and institutions. Whenever I mention the corporation, company, business, institution, or organization, I am referring to any public or private business entity or agency that has extensive data operations. Furthermore, unless otherwise noted, whenever I mention the industry I'm speaking to all business types and the data operations within them.

Most examples I present in this book are firsthand accounts where I was personally involved and privy to project and program details shared by clients and prospects as well as information and experiences discovered during the course of numerous engagements. These illustrations are primarily of United States-based companies, most with international operations. However, you will find plenty of examples covering other countries, the public sector, and nearly every industry vertical.

Though the title of this book implies that that it was written exclusively for upper management it is actually geared to any audience interested in the topic. For executives, decision makers, and business leaders it is an ideal way to understand data governance in business terms that you can relate to. For stakeholders, architects, business and technology leads it is a means for better understanding data governance holistically, the value it brings to the business, and to learn how to build a compelling business case in the process. For data stewards and other participants it is an excellent way to understand the concepts and value around data governance and how each person's role supports the process.

This book is not your typical technology manuscript and if you find it to be then I have not accomplished what I set out to do. Rather than speak exclusively to bits, bytes, and attributes I've written about how people, process, technology, business, culture, and political alignment can and must work together to drive business performance in the world of data and information management.

To some folks it may appear that I have a tendency to pick on the information technology (IT) organization since I use multiple and sometimes faultfinding examples that involve this great professional institution. My intentions are not to embarrass or degrade the group in any way. Instead, I have tried to shed light on the unreasonable expectations that have been placed on IT over time and their consequences. Let there be no doubt about the enormous contribution IT has made and continues to make to the data management and governance community.

Keep in mind that a good portion of this book is about building a platform or framework for data governance to prosper. Data governance in and of itself does not solve data management problems but rather positions organizations to confront and resolve the issues they face. Once in place this platform can and should be a powerful force in providing direction, identifying opportunities and challenges, setting priorities, developing solutions, enforcing accountability, resolving issues, and taking business performance to the next level by optimizing data and information assets.

This book also is about taking a top down approach to data governance, which should not be confused with 'boiling the ocean'. There are a number of creative ways to successfully position data governance at a high level in the company yet roll it out on a graduated, project-by-project basis. The important thing is to create a living, breathing program that can transcend multiple projects, and whose lifecycle does not end at the conclusion of a project.

While I admire bottom up and grassroots initiatives, they come with clear limitations, restricted scope, and high rates of failure. Those programs that experience some level of success seldom grow into what everyone envisions. Finally, you will not find anything in this book that talks to the practice of non-invasive data governance. The discipline of governance is as much about changing process, behaviors, and culture as anything so it has to have an invasive element to it in order to drive success and optimize business performance.

My hope is that you will find this book to offer an insightful if not refreshing perspective into data governance as well as provide powerful, practical solutions for achieving success in the complex world of enterprise information asset management. More importantly, I hope it plants the seeds for reflection, new ideas, innovation, and growth in order to advance the discipline within your organization and the industry.

Enjoy and good luck in your endeavors.

James C. Orr

Chapter 1

Background

Data – A unique and extremely complex asset

Data is the most unique asset in your organization. Unlike traditional assets, data is exceptionally dynamic and can change its physical characteristics, logical characteristics, value, and ownership at indiscriminate points in time. Additionally, data encounters the broadest range of influencers throughout its lifecycle. The transformations that occur at the hands of these influential factors ultimately determine the usability and value of the information.

Perhaps its most distinctive characteristic is that data is fluid. Fluid in the sense that it passes through multiple people, processes, technologies, business units, organization structures, and cultures from the time it originates in the organization until it is consumed for business purposes. During its life cycle, data engages various so-called owners, users, responsible parties, casual bystanders, good intentions, and blurred lines of authority and accountability. In each case, these touch-points have an opportunity to either improve or deplete the value of data based on their actions or inactions.

This dynamic ecosystem is what gives data its well-earned designation as a living asset. Much like a living organism its behavior, health, growth, and potential are highly influenced by a number of ongoing environmental factors. This alone makes it arguably the most difficult asset to understand and manage. Its distinctive makeup incorporates several other characteristics and circumstances that contribute to its intricacy. The complexity stems from multiple;

- Owners
- Consumers
- Systems
- Sources
- Storage locations
- Formats
- Attributes
- Data types
- Relationships
- Business units
- Companies
- Business functions
- Business processes
- Languages
- Data models/architectures
- Data definitions
- Technologies

What makes the data ecosystem even more elaborate is that these characteristics and influencers are heavily interdependent of one another yet they persist in silo environments. This means the value of your company data is directly proportional to the ability of the business to organize, synchronize, and manage these facets of the data environment in a way that breeds continuity, collaboration, and accountability across the continuum of the data and information life cycle.

You don't know what you don't know!

One thing the industry has taught us about data and information is that their greatest influence on the business lies hidden beneath the surface of day-to-day operations. The sheer intricacy of the data environment shields us from realizing the full impact of these assets and subsequently the opportunities, risk, and value concealed within it. This is supported by countless case studies, surveys, testimonials, and real life examples brought forth by organizations and industry professionals around the world. The most noteworthy being the hidden financial impact data has on a company's bottom line.

"On average, companies estimate they are losing $8.2 million dollars annually because of data quality issues with 22% of businesses estimating losses over $20 million per year."

Gartner Group[1]

"On average, companies estimate they lose over $5 million dollars annually due to data related problems with 20% of businesses estimating losses over $20 million per year."

Forbes Insights [2]

When it comes to the Gartner Study the bigger surprise may be that more than 50 percent of the organizations surveyed reported that they had no idea how much money they are losing, which underscores the notion that companies don't know what they don't know.

The Forbes Insights study goes on to say that *"fragmented ownership is the single biggest roadblock to an enterprise information management program."*

---

[1] Gartner Inc., *Findings From Primary Research Study: Organizations Perceive Significant Cost Impact From Data Quality Issues,* Ted Friedman, August 14, 2009.
(http://www.gartner.com/DisplayDocument?id=1131012)

[2] Forbes Insights in association with SAP, *Managing Information in the Enterprise: Perspectives for Business Leaders,* April 2010.
(http://images.forbes.com/forbesinsights/StudyPDFs/SAP_InformationManagement_04_2010.pdf)

Poorly drawn data boundaries and ill-conceived lienholder rights are certainly a leading contributor to the overall problem. We will dive into the details behind this and the financial impact of data governance in subsequent chapters; but for the sake of discussion, assume you fall into the category of a company that is experiencing material financial loss from this cancerous condition, and chances are you do.

Now before you go off and fire your CIO and the entire IT staff keep in mind that there are some very rational explanations as to why you are in this mess. Yes, this is your mess, too! In fact it might be more your mess than anyone else if you are in a position to fix it.

Why hasn't anyone mentioned this to you? Well, there are a number of reasons but primarily because no one group or individual within your organization has the access or visibility into everything they need to see in order to fully understand and depict the entire picture. In reality, most of the picture is below the surface and invisible to the organization.

Yes, some pockets in the company such as IT are more aware of problems than others but even their interpretation of the predicament is narrow in focus, project based, and normally measured in technical and/or operational metrics rather than in business terms. Besides, if IT raised the flag too high someone might take things the wrong way and question their historical performance in managing data. In reality it is not about any one group or individual's aptitude, it is about an industry that over time has adopted not-so-best best practices when it comes to data and information asset management.

How did we get into this mess?

A number of events and practices have transpired over the years which have led to the costly data management challenges we see today. With few exceptions, no single proceeding is responsible for the problem at hand but rather all of these together have contributed to the evolution of the complex data environments we have come to know. The circumstances created by these events are outpacing our ability to respond to the problems that they stem from.

System and Intellectual Fragmentation

Do you ever long for the days when companies ran their business on a couple core mainframe technology systems with a small team of people that knew everything about those systems? One can argue the merits of legacy technologies but who can quarrel with how much easier and straightforward it was to manage the data? I didn't say better, just simpler. For the most part the technology, data, and intellectual property were in one physical and logical location! Does it get any sweeter?

Today the world is far more complex and disjointed. The number of systems and technologies used by businesses has multiplied exponentially, and will continue to grow by all accounts. Subject matter expertise is spread thin across companies with experts reporting to various business units with different or conflicting priorities. Data volumes continue to grow at rates known to double every 18-24 months giving rise to more "Big Data" environments. Software as a service (SaaS), Cloud computing, and outsourced data management functions further distance companies from managing and controlling their own data. Expanded partnerships with manufacturers, distributors, resellers, and agencies have increased the number of data sources and challenges that go with it. Global expansion, especially non-organic via merger and acquisition, has presented another set of data obstacles.

Over time, this fragmented data environment has been shaped by a number of reasonable and not-so-reasonable technical and business practices.

Technology Advancement
- Migration from legacy to open systems
- Relational databases
- Proliferation of desktop applications
- Internet
- Web-based applications
- E-mail
- Software as a Service (SaaS)
- Cloud computing
- Advent of specialized business applications and solutions
    - Enterprise data warehouse (EDW)
    - Data warehouse (DW)
    - Operational data store (ODS)

- Data marts
- Customer relationship master (CRM)
- Customer data integration (CDI)
- Enterprise resource planning (ERP)
- Business intelligence (BI)
- Master data management (MDM)
- Data quality (DQ)
- Sales management
- Campaign management
- Call center management
- Financial management
- Resource management
- Asset management
- Materials management
- Human resource management
- Work flow management
- Policy management
- Contract management
- Records management
- Content management

Business Events and Ideology

- Merger and acquisition (M&A)
- Business partnerships (manufacturers, distributors, resellers, agencies)
- Globalization (language and culture)
- Reorganization (frequency and magnitude)
- In-house vs. outsource vs. off shore (data management activities)
- Centralization vs. decentralization
- Individual incentives incompatible with the organization's best interests

Regulation and Compliance

- Government
- Industry specific
- Trade specific
- Consumer privacy
- Financial
- Healthcare

Although the industry has pushed hard to streamline business and develop flexible, specialized solutions using the latest and greatest technology, it has left in its wake what seems for many as an overwhelming challenge: to effectively manage data across so many people, processes, and systems.

While there are multiple illustrations of fragmentation, there is no better way to corroborate this concept then when I inevitably ask organizations a few questions beginning with the following one that I put in front of both IT and the business:

"Which group or individuals within your company understands the complete life cycle of your data from start to finish?"

In other words, where and how is data created and entered, where is it stored, where and how is it integrated, who owns the data, what are the relationships to other data, what does it mean, and how is it used by the business? With the exception of financial data, over 90 percent of the answers I receive are that nobody in the organization understands the entire data life cycle. For those that claim they do have a grasp on their data environment, it normally comes down to one or two people that have that level of knowledge.

For those companies that answer "yes" to my first question, I follow up with this question:

"Is your data life cycle documented?"

Almost every company I have ever asked this question of has answered "no." In fact, most go on to say that there is minimal or no metadata available on their data environment. This supports the universal concern I hear over and over by business units, which is: who owns the data, how do I get it, and how do I know it is correct?

The third and last question I pose, in this case to IT specifically, is as follows:

"Do you understand where and how data is used by the business?"

Now this question always sparks interesting responses and conversation. If the audience is made up solely of IT professionals, they are normally quick to puff up their chests and say "yes." That is until I probe deeper and find out they have never actually sat down with the business to discuss and/or observed how the data is consumed. In many cases the IT folks don't even know the people on the business side let alone understand what they do and how they do it.

I once did data governance work for a financial institution that involved conducting interviews of 10 IT and 22 business personnel. The IT stakeholder was a very talented and knowledgeable person who had been with the company for a number of years. This individual requested to be present during the business interviews, which I obliged. Of the 22 people we met with, the IT stakeholder met 19 of them for the very first time and conducted a fair amount of data troubleshooting on the spot.

Unfortunately, this is not an isolated instance. I find that the vast majority of IT people only see the tip of the iceberg when it comes to how the business actually consumes the data. The same can be said for the business people that typically have even less understanding of how IT interacts with data. In both cases the insight and span of influence of these groups is determined by the level of fragmentation within their data and work environment.

Having spent a good number of years in the software vendor and consulting space I always enjoy swapping stories and experiences with people that have worked in similar capacities in CRM, BI, DQ, DW, MDM, CDI, and other related areas. Behind closed doors my constituents and I always find consensus in the fact that companies rarely understand or take the time to comprehend the impact data and information has on their overall business. For those that do the experience is a game changer, if they choose to act.

These collective experiences not only validate the persistence of system and intellectual fragmentation within companies but they also expose how hideous it is to think that a single person, IT group, or loosely knit team can effectively make sound business decisions around data assets. It also goes back to the point – you don't know what you don't know, and in the data management world we don't know what we don't know.

Project vs. Program Based Budgeting

A principal reason the industry has created a mess for itself is the way organizations budget at a project versus a program level. Though project based budgeting works well for most business initiatives, it hardly serves as a data manager's best friend. This practice and the ramifications from it are well known by anyone who has worked in the data management space for any length of time.

The most significant impact of project based budgeting is that once the project is complete many data management activities come to a halt. This clashes with the very nature of data in that data has a never-ending life cycle. Any gains made during the project are often lost.

Another consequence of project based budgeting is that data outcomes are dependent on coordinating upstream, downstream, and lateral data management activities around people, process, technology, and lines of business. Project based budgets only deal with a subset of the overall picture and ignore the end-to-end data life cycle. For example, most companies that budget for a data warehouse do not take into account all the data management activities associated with the source systems and processes that feed the data warehouse. This often results in the same garbage data moving from source systems to the data warehouse.

Project based budgeting also permits business units to plan in a vacuum. All too often this results in a plan that does not take into account the business, technical, and data management interconnectivity necessary to drive successful results. Data governance initiatives can be applied at a project layer but the discipline itself needs to be set up as an independent program that transcends all data intensive projects in order to abolish the silo effect and drive business performance.

A large banking institution once shared with me that they felt they did a great job with BI, CRM and DW. In fact, they were very proud of their staff, their skills, and their ability to execute. However, all their efforts up to that point had been conducted in project silos with no overarching data management strategy. Despite their aptitude, their project based culture had left the company with several independent systems, multiple cross-functional data quality issues, and the inability to demonstrate a 360 degree view of their customers.

Unreasonable Expectation and Practices of IT Ownership

Over time the industry has adopted the notion that IT owns all aspects of data and information management. After all, it is their systems that process, manage, store, and report on company data. This approach has created a few problems, one being that IT has become out of touch with the business and vice versa. Another is that IT is held accountable for many data related challenges that are out of their control. Yet another is that this framework has served as a platform for some IT organizations to exercise unhealthy and unreasonable power and control within their company.

Today, most data decisions are still made in a vacuum at an IT project layer without the necessary input from the business. This practice serves short-term interests (just get it done!) while creating long-term consequences. The apprehension for IT to connect with the business is often the result of age-old expectations and attitudes that the responsibility falls entirely to IT. Complicating the issue is the alarming number of IT organizations that simply do not know who or what the business really is. This arms length relationship is often fueled by the business that may not want to be bothered, does not have the time, and after all isn't it an IT responsibility?

The challenge with this approach is that IT cannot possibly deliver to the expectations of the business without collaborative participation in establishing and managing business rules, data standards, and business process among other things. Just look to the failed data intensive projects of the past (i.e., CRM, BI, EDW, Data Marts, CDI, etc.). In those initiatives where outcomes fall short of expectations, companies will commonly point the finger at the software vendor and/or their IT organization. In reality, it has everything to do with the lack of global data strategies and the collaboration of business and IT to solve these business problems. To their credit, a number of IT shops are beginning to stand up to the business and demanding participation in order to establish mutual expectations and drive desired data outcomes. Essentially, telling the business that technology alone and IT by itself do not fix the problems.

Several years ago someone told me that IT people think they can do anything. Their statement was targeted not so much at IT professionals but rather the unsavory situations the industry has created for itself when IT is given carte blanche to create solutions on their own accord. While I admire the creativity of IT professionals, I have also witnessed a concerning number of situations where IT is given the rule of the roost without any collaboration or vetting process by people in the business. Such practices are destined for failure when it comes to data. With excessive power comes an unhealthy arrogance (ignorance?) that can cost organizations significant amounts of time and money. While not the norm, these situations are not uncommon either.

It takes both business and IT to drive quality outcomes. While the lines of responsibility may not always be clear neither party should be held to an unreasonable, if not disproportionate, standard of responsibility. Both parties also should be given the benefit of the doubt since these situations have been shaped by years of false expectations and not from the negligence of any one individual or group.

Data governance instills the weights, balances, and accountability needed to make this happen.

Migration from Legacy to Open System/Relational Databases

For all the perceived shortcomings of legacy technology systems, they do a few things very well. Perhaps the principal benefit is that they store data in a centralized location where it was easily managed and understood. The advent of relational databases and highly specialized software applications has distributed data, information, and intellectual property across multiple systems, databases, and lines of business.

Data governance helps organizations identify, recapture, and coordinate the data and intellectual property that has been diluted through this technology evolution.

Merger and Acquisition (M&A)

For most companies the process of migrating data from merger and acquisition activities is seldom thought out to the appropriate level of detail. In fact it normally follows the path of "we bought XYZ Corp today; we need to merge their data with ours by the end of the quarter. I don't care how you do it, just get it done." The problem with this approach is that it introduces lingering, long-term issues that range from poor data quality, to duplication of information, to loading obsolete data, to the lack of data standards. All of which create significant downstream business problems across the board.

From a business perspective, this approach is not likely to change, nor should it. After all, the organization is making this move in order to grow overall company revenues as quickly as possible. The role of data governance is to better represent and prepare the organization to make smarter short and long-term decisions around the data before it is merged in the limited time that is available.

Perpetual Corporate Reorganization

The industry has made a number of valiant attempts to start data governance only to be stopped in their tracks with the next corporate reorganization. The revolving door has stopped a number of really good initiatives. A well-defined and well-structured data governance presence can reverse this trend every time someone at the top sneezes.

Chapter Summary

While it is important to understand where we have been and what we are dealing with in order to get to where we need to go, it is even more important that we steer our focus toward solving the data and information management dilemmas that face us. Before we go further, let me say that there is no silver bullet answer to these challenges. Moreover, technology cannot begin to fix all this. Don't get me wrong, technology plays a very important role but the answer to managing data assets is about implementing an information asset management or data governance practice that can begin to globally manage and coordinate the people, process, technology, and business alignment required to address these issues and optimize business performance.

Just like technology, data governance cannot possibly solve every data and information problem that the organization faces. In fact, your company may need to come to the realization that some problems cannot be cured; but the symptoms can be managed. What data governance does is position the organization to begin to wrap its arms around the issues and start making responsible, business minded decisions around data assets that benefit the overall health and well-being of the organization.

Chapter 2

Data Governance – What is it?

Overview

Let me start by doing what so many people try to do, which is to encapsulate the essence of data governance in a single paragraph definition.

"Data governance is the discipline of administering data and information assets across an organization through formal oversight of the people,

processes, technologies, and lines of business that influence data and informational outcomes to drive business performance."

Whether you happen to like this definition or not there is no significance to this characterization until one puts it into context. A few simple sentences cannot possibly convey the scope and complexity of data governance. A contextual discussion of data governance allows one to appreciate why so many organizations have a different slant and scope on this discipline. Perhaps most important, with further insight you can begin to visualize the potential far-reaching impact this discipline can have across an organization.

The term data governance symbolizes different things to different people, groups, professions, organizations, and industries. So diverse are the definitions that the industry is in the midst of redefining this discipline as the ink dries on this book. While the concept of governance makes complete sense in the world of data and information management, the scope, oversight, and application of it is sometimes off the charts.

If you speak with a data architect, chances are his or her governance definition and requirements will be tech heavy and pertain primarily to data models, technical integration of data policy, and possibly data structures within a single project. Chief architects or technical project managers may have a slightly broader interpretation that includes data ownership rights, metadata management, and workflow management between disparate work groups and systems. Subject matter experts (SMEs) may define data governance with regard to data quality, fixing data, and tactical management of duplicate data. Business managers commonly will articulate the need for data standards, stewardship, and business process. Once you venture into middle and upper management, data governance begins to take on more of a business connotation. The problem, as you may be beginning to see, is that data governance exists in all of these capacities within an organization, but is seldom presented holistically to executive management.

Further complicating the depiction of this discipline are the overlapping and converging practices that have evolved over the years, such as Enterprise Information Management (EIM), Enterprise Content Management (ECM), Records Management (RM), Master Data Management (MDM), Enterprise Risk Management (ERM), Personal Information Management (PIM), IT Governance, BI Governance, and others. In some cases these initiatives are being rolled up into or under Business Process Management (BPM), Business Transformation and other process improvement endeavors. Where each one starts and stops would confuse most individuals let alone the CxO…and it often does!

Essentially, each of these practices is attempting to tackle the same problems as that of data governance; however, each touts different origins, followers, and specific areas of focus. Individually they make for good intentions by attempting to get their arms around corporate management of data and information assets but each falls short of what is needed to manage the full data and information life cycle.

Data governance is not about creating another renegade discipline to add to bureaucratic overhead. In part, it is about strengthening the many concepts and practices that have grown out of similar endeavors. It also is about eliminating duplicate efforts within the organization and formally coordinating common activities between various interest groups for driving business performance. For some organizations, this will be an entirely new venture built from scratch. For others it means taking preexisting projects and responsibilities and consolidating them under a formal data governance umbrella. Yet for others it may reflect an ecosystem where data disciplines coexist under a more formal, centralized, collaborative, and productive data management environment.

We will cover the relationships between these analogous domains in more detail in Chapter 9 on organizational structure and alignment. Until then, it is important to note that this seemingly competitive environment for control of company data and information assets can only be orchestrated through a formal and comprehensive business process.

Data governance grew out of the technology ranks where the earliest concepts of managing data go back several years. IT professionals are known to say: "We have been doing data governance for years; we just didn't call it that." To a certain extent, they are exactly right. Correct in the sense that they have tried to address some strategic but mostly tactical and technical aspects of data governance on a project-by-project basis over the years as time and budgets would permit. Most initial efforts were centered on technical design around data models, naming conventions, attributes, data types, data formats, and some level of data standardization. In most cases, data decisions were made by IT within a single project using their best judgment. While many recognized the need for things like metadata, data quality, governance, and collaboration between systems and business, their voices were seldom heard, as a result, generally accepted yet not so best-best practices prevailed.

Since the early days of technical tinkering, data governance has morphed into something far more expansive and diverse over the last few years. Today it is as much about establishing and administering corporate level oversight of data assets and getting the business involved in the process as it is advancing the technical implementation of data governance within existing and new technologies. Many in the industry, me included, believe it is far more about business process redesign, change management, and/or business process management than it is about technology.

So what changed the landscape? One could endlessly debate the answers to this question but the principal drivers for bringing data governance to the forefront is today's competitive business environment. Organizations are clamoring to develop 360 degree or enterprise views of their business to stay competitive, reduce risk, and drive compliance. This involves linking information across disparate systems that were never intended to talk to each other technically or operationally. In order to achieve this holistic view organizations recognize they must instill a business process that accounts for corporate oversight of data. While technology remains an important ingredient, organizations can no longer lean on technology alone to drive the business results they are expecting when it comes to their data.

As data governance has evolved, it has begun to test the relevance of its very name. The primary challenge to this title is the false perception it emits within the business and executive communities. In the eyes of the business world the word 'data' typically points to bits, bytes, tactical, and technical centric data management activities where IT has full ownership and responsibility. As for the word 'governance', it is commonly interpreted as another layer of bureaucracy, overhead, and cost. Adding fuel to the fire, there is nothing in the name of this discipline that reflects the value or importance that could elevate its stature in the organization. Collectively this does not bode well for a discipline that is working to influence the business and expand its footprint across the enterprise. In fact, the term has been known to have unintended consequences in certain organizations where it prevents the practice from prospering.

When data governance was a technically based discipline, the term was appropriate. However, the discipline has evolved and the term no longer represents the sum of its parts. After all, think about other asset management divisions within an organization, such as financial management/services, human resources, materials management, or asset management. We would never refer to these activities as *money governance, people governance, inventory governance,* or *asset governance,* respectively. While governing is an important aspect to each of these disciplines, the terms data and governance no longer adequately describes their core function and purpose.

So what do we call it? I think data governance is more to do with something I refer to as 'Enterprise Information Asset Management' (EIAM). The term itself is simple, self-descriptive, practical, all-inclusive, non-threatening and more likely to fit within the mainstream of an organization's structure and political climate. Besides, it gives data governance its rightful place among other asset management entities and satisfies industry demands to treat data like an asset. While I'd like to debate the logic and anoint the terminology to a new industry standard the fact of the matter is that it is still called data governance today, so I'll go with the flow for now. Nevertheless, I can only hope that the industries will self-correct and move toward Enterprise Information Asset Management in the near future.

Now that we have established the nomenclature, just what is Enterprise Information Asset Management...I mean, data governance? As I alluded to earlier, at the end of the day it is about formally organizing and managing data and information assets across and organization from a technical, business, and administrative perspective in order to optimize data and business outcomes.

The Influencers

A good exercise in understanding data governance and its scope is to examine the primary activities and practices that materially influence data and informational outcomes, both good and bad. These consist of five basic categories.

1) Data management operations
2) Technology
3) Business process
4) Organization policy
5) Culture

By understanding what influences the condition and livelihood of these assets one can better recognize what requires governance.

Data Management Operations as an Influencer

At the center of data management are a number of specialty domains, sub-domains, and activities that influence data outcomes and require orchestration through a centralized governing body. Some of these domains are technology centric, others business focused, yet others have varying levels of overlap between the two. Here are the most common data management domains that organizations embrace today.

- Data quality
- Data modeling
- Data integration
- Data security and privacy
- Data stewardship
- Data standards
- Data lineage
- Data analytics
- Metadata management
- Business rules
- Data policy
- Work flow management
- Monitoring, measuring, trending, and reporting

Of all these domains, data quality may arguably receive the most attention, which explains why some organizations refer to data quality and data governance as being one-in-the-same. However, while they do have striking similarities that we will discuss further in subsequent chapters, these are two distinct and separate disciplines with data quality being a sub-discipline of data governance. This holds true for each of the other data management domains as well. Each are considered sub-domains under the overarching data governance umbrella.

Most groups responsible for data management operations are more inclined to focus on implementing the technologies they manage than dealing with the broader data governance concerns. These domains normally dedicate just enough time to data governance policymaking to implement the technology. Most policymaking initiatives within a domain barely scratch the surface and are commonly restricted to business rule development for a single project. Because of this, a data management function should never be considered data governance in its own right. Rather, data governance is a formal body that creates and oversees the collective data strategies and data policies of each of these domains together.

I always find my first conversation with an organization interesting, as I never know what I will hear when the discussion shifts to the topic of data governance. Over the years I have heard some fascinating definitions and requirements for governance, some strategic, most tactical and technical, and nearly all aligning themselves closely with one or more of the previously described sub-domains. In many instances, organizations indicate they are looking to achieve data governance but in reality don't know what they want until the possibilities are actually explained to them.

To better illustrate the basic framework of data governance from a data management perspective it is good to have visibility into the relationship between influential data management functions, data and information types, and projects (Figure 2.1). This diagram simply shows what is possible for data governance within the data management space and not what is required. Organizations do not need to boil the ocean but do need to be aware of how this discipline can scale across various projects, data domains, and data management functions.

Working from right to left in Figure 2.1, data governance normally attaches itself to an initial project and then expands over time to incorporate other projects. As you can see, the list of potential projects that involve data governance is extensive. The scope and opportunities for data management further expand when organizations incorporate various data domains. The projects and data domains involved normally determine which data management functions come into play in order to optimize the value of the data for the project's success.

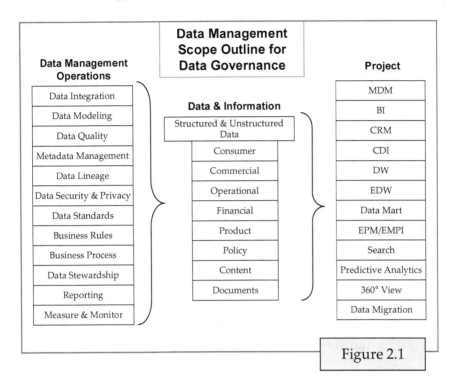

Figure 2.1

The reach of a data governance program will vary from one organization to the next with the most practical starting with a single project, one data domain, and two to four data management functions. For example, a data warehouse project may deal strictly with consumer data, data integration, data quality, and data standards as a starting point. Few if any of these initiatives are ever the same even if they look the same on paper. As time and success build, the span of control of a data governance program can extend to a number of other projects, data types, data management functions, and lines of business.

Technology as an Influencer

Technologies directly influence data and informational outcomes through their capacity to implement and automate data policies that come from business requirements. Technologies that can effectively facilitate these policies and collectively present accurate information at the right time and for the right reason have a powerful influence on data and informational outcomes and subsequent business performance. The extents to which technologies can apply data policies to automatic processes determine whether the tools become either an enabler or obstacle to business performance.

Given the role technology plays in data outcomes, it is important to take a moment to better understand the fundamental task technology has in data governance as well as clarify some common misconceptions that go with it.

- Technology is an enabler not a creator of data governance policy.

- Technology implements and automates data policy established by the data governance process.

- The most frequent automated data policies involve an assortment of business rules, standards, and work flows. The business is responsible for creating data policy. Once established the policy is implemented to various degrees across a number of software technologies. Common technologies that attempt to incorporate these policies include data quality, data integration, data modeling, metadata management, and core software applications such as MDM, CRM, EDW, DW, BI, and ERP.

- No single technology can possibly automate every aspect of data governance.

One of the biggest challenges organizations face is to understand which data governance technologies and capabilities are needed and why? We will answer these and other technology questions in Chapter 10. Until then it is important to note that technology can be confusing given that in recent years nearly every traditional technology provider seems to attest to the fact that their technology does data governance. Well, what does that really mean? Have software vendors truly developed new data governance capabilities, repurposed existing technology, or are they simply re-branding their software to embrace the industry buzz around data governance? Moreover, what part of data governance do they actually do?

This book does not intend to make your software selections for you; but it is important to understand some of the minefields that are out there. Data governance remains a relatively immature industry. For technology, this means there are some early adopter vendors making creative and incremental improvements to their products by accommodating new, sophisticated forms of data governance automation. On the other hand, many are simply re-branding existing technologies to take advantage of the industry buzz. You are obviously the judge and the jury on this; but I would encourage every organization to examine what technology providers mean when they tout that they do data governance. Understanding technology capabilities around data governance at a project and enterprise level can mean the difference between success and failure.

The Customer Relationship Master (CRM) software industry is a great example of how technology influences data outcomes in both a good and bad way. The technologies in this space add value to organizations when it comes to organizing and managing customer accounts, sales activity, leads, contacts, pipelines, and so forth. At the same time, CRM applications are prone to what could be the worst possible data problem; duplicate records. Repetitive records clearly inhibit an organization when it comes to rolling up information, conducting marketing campaigns, and opening up customer portals to access the data.

One reason for this is that for many years CRM applications had little if any data quality capabilities, including the ability to identify and merge duplicate entries. Many still do not. Even if an organization had well-defined data governance policies around CRM, the applications were limited in their ability to implement the policies and duplicate information continued to persist. While some CRM vendors have made improvements in this area the fact remains that record duplication can be a serious problem with these solutions.

For organizations that have implemented CRM, many have found that record duplication has prevented them from leveraging the information to their initial expectations. Not only has this diluted anticipated returns on investment but it also has increased costs as many companies have created expensive data warehouses and funded custom solutions in an attempt to circumvent the data duplication problem.

My point is not to encourage you to throw away your CRM solution or scratch any plans for a new one. On the contrary, despite the record duplication issues, CRM is known to provide significant benefit to business operations. The point is that technologies such as this clearly influence data outcomes and business performance in unexpected ways. It is utterly important for organizations to understand how technologies of this nature govern data quality, record duplication, and data remediation in order to protect long-term investments and optimize business performance.

When it comes to data governance and technology, it is imperative that the business and IT are working closely together as reflected in Figure 2.2. For the business, it means immersing themselves into the process of defining and managing business rules, standards, workflows, and other required data policies. For technologist, it is to be proactive in helping the business understand software capabilities and specifically how data policies can or cannot effectively map to them.

We will explore the relationship between business and IT in more detail later in this and subsequent chapters. The important thing to note is that both camps need to collaborate on how software providers account for data governance within their applications and then develop effective data strategies around these capabilities.

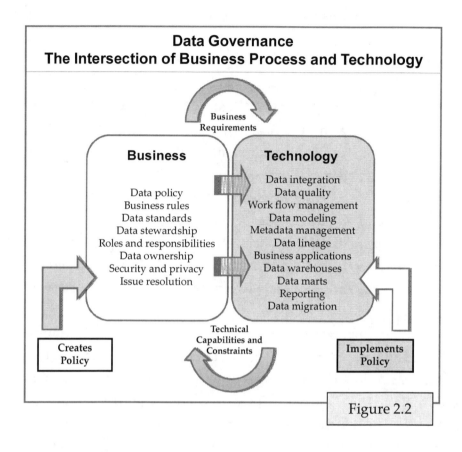

Figure 2.2

It is critical for organizations to adopt these practices for every data centric project in order to overcome historical practices that are detrimental to the health and well-being of data assets. Organizations need to rid themselves from silo decision making and attach an overarching data management strategy to technology selection and implementation. Collectively it requires a data governance body to contribute to, if not facilitate these activities.

Business Process as an Influencer

Business process influences a variety of data and information outcomes. Some of the most common examples of this involve data entry and collection practices, data aggregation, reporting, data reconciliation, data enrichment, data remediation, data analysis, and work flow management. Bad business processes can lead directly to data errors, which negatively affect the business, or render perfectly good information unusable.

One common example of this is how organizations add new customers, prospects, members, or clients to their system. The on-boarding process can come through a number of channels to include online purchases, electronic membership applications, requests for information via the Internet, manual paper forms, telephone solicitation and inquiries, and merger and acquisition. For some organizations, it can mean all of the above with processes also extending to partners and resellers in the business-to-business (B2B) environment.

In many instances, these points of entry are void of the necessary controls to accurately record and validate information. In other circumstances, the controls are inconsistently applied because business process is absent or not followed. This sort of environment leads to problems with missing and inaccurate data and, worst of all, duplicate records. While the initial business purpose may be met, subsequent business, such as sales, renewals, marketing, billing, and customer service can suffer significantly from these practices.

Another example of business process run amok is how organizations have disparate systems that do not interface with each other. In those situations, companies have to rely on business process to compare information between systems. A good illustration of this is how the mortgage industry recently found itself foreclosing and even auctioning off homes that homeowners still rightfully owned. Known as Foreclosuregate, this mortgage industry crisis is about questionable, if not fraudulent, practices within financial institutions when processing home foreclosures.

Questionable behaviors aside, a contributing factor to Foreclosuregate is that organizations did not have the information they needed to process the foreclosure transactions. In the absence of technology, the institutions had to rely on business process to produce the correct business outcomes. Unfortunately, the business process was inadequate and led to a number of incorrect foreclosures, lawsuits, and federal investigations into the practices of several financial institutions.

Business process clearly affects data and business outcomes. Data governance can play an instrumental role in identifying and managing business process opportunities.

Organization Policy as an Influencer

Organization policy is one of the most significant contributors to data and information outcomes. There are countless examples where subliminal and often naive corporate decisions negatively influence downstream data outcomes. These actions frequently take place without data governance having a seat at the table to help educate policymakers and guide the organization's data strategy. To reverse this practice data governance will have to play an active role in corporate policymaking.

As a data governance program matures, its leadership should have the authority, aptitude, and visibility to guide a broad range of directives around enterprise data and information management. These directives can involve a number of topics that are normally off limits for many organizations today.

- Customer definition
- Merger and acquisition
- Project and budgetary planning
- Technology selection
- Data enrichment
- Business partner integration
- Data security and privacy
- Risk and compliance
- Business partner integration
- Global standards
- Center of Excellence (CoE)

A data governance program should be directly involved in establishing corporate and agency policy in order to influence positive data outcomes.

Culture as an Influencer

Culture clearly dictates the success of many business activities within an organization. When it comes to persuading an organization to treat data as an asset rather than data as a commodity, there are no exceptions to the rule. Business traditions continue to affect data outcomes and in ways that touch on data ownership rights, accountability, project planning, business verses IT, political barriers, business process, data life cycle management, and much more.

Cultures never change overnight and in order to move the status quo it requires a strong change agent. Data governance is just that vehicle. It provides the platform to invoke sensible business processes and actionable results across the organization.

Three Operational Components to Data Governance

We will discuss the three operational components to data governance throughout this book; however, this is a good point to pause and introduce this fundamental concept. By doing so, it should help you visualize how data governance organizes itself to drive business performance.

The three operational components to governance consist of business, technical, and administrative functions. Though interdependent, each is very different, serves a specific purpose, and requires a different set of people and skills to implement. Figure 2.3 illustrates these components.

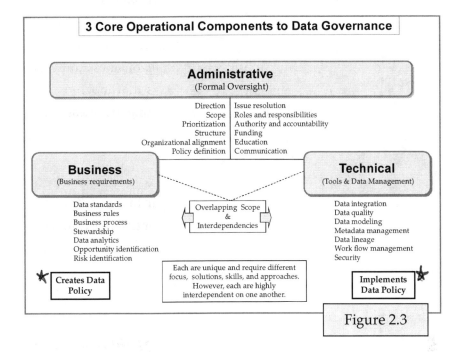

Figure 2.3

1) **Administrative Data Governance** – Represents the administrative body necessary to oversee the entire data governance program. The primary focus is on strategy, direction, policy, business alignment, issue resolution, and other oversight responsibilities. This is normally led by business with sound representation from IT and business leadership.

2) **Technical Data Governance** – Represents governance activities that are technology centric and can include areas such as data modeling, metadata management, data integration, and other technology heavy data management

domains. These activities are led by technologists and have a direct or indirect responsibility to the administrative data governance body.

3) **Business Data Governance** – Represents business centric activities such as data standards, business process, business rules, stewardship, and more. These activities should be business led and operate under the direction of the administrative data governance body.

The purpose of this exercise is not to introduce three separate data governance initiatives but rather to distinguish between vital governance functions within a single program. One of the most common references in this mix is how business and IT need to work together as a team since they have overlapping governing roles and responsibilities. For example, a key differentiator in untangling joint responsibilities is recognizing that the business is accountable in principal for establishing rules, policy, standards, and requirements while IT is responsible for governing the implementation of those decisions within the technologies.

The third dimension to this equation is clearly the most important yet; shockingly, also the most overlooked. Administrative data governance is the foundation of any successful governance program, especially those that have enterprise or data life cycle aspirations attached to it. Organizations that do not take the time to clearly define, differentiate, position, and empower the administrative arm of a data governance program will not achieve their goals and objectives. Grassroots efforts are a testament to this. These ambitious and admirable initiatives lack the formal administrative component necessary to be successful beyond a single project (if at all) or to scale their program going forward.

We will expand upon the three operational components of governance throughout the book. Until then, this should provide enough background to enhance your understanding of what comprises data governance as well as the necessary building blocks for success.

High Performance Programs

When data governance programs are running on all cylinders, they provide the organization solid leadership, optimize business performance, and supply a platform for which to develop and strengthen a number of corporate data strategies, policies, and procedures that are either non-existent today or simply in need of help.

A high performance program will possess many of the following characteristics.

- A strong administrative arm
- A healthy span of control over a number of data management functions
- Representation in or control over a number of corporate data policies
- Involvement with multiple data types and domains
- Extend influence across an entire data life cycle and/or the enterprise
- Contain a Center of Excellence or competency center

Additionally, the program becomes the go-to for all data related initiatives and challenges that arise; therefore providing the company the agility they need to respond to crisis and opportunities. Finally, as the data governance program matures it becomes the change agent for modifying historical cultural practices across lines of business and technologies.

What is the Point?

Why is data governance so important? Simply stated, it drives optimal data outcomes not achievable under normal business operations. Consequently, these outcomes become business benefits that reflect positively in the company's overall financial performance (Figure 2.4).

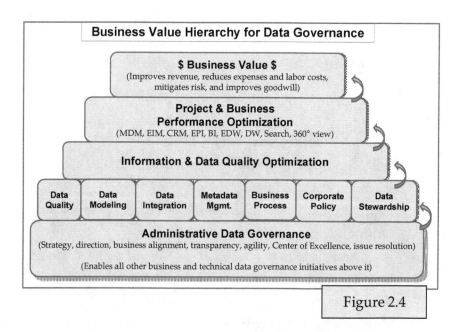

Figure 2.4

In order to optimize business value, successful programs must begin with a solid administrative data governance footprint, which enables a number of data management domains to flourish across the enterprise. In turn, it optimizes the quality of the data and information in support of data intensive projects. Finally, by optimizing the data outcomes for projects it maximizes the business value and the return on investment of data governance and the projects it supports.

The most valuable concept to understand about this high-level model is that successful data governance requires a building block approach that begins with a solid administrative arm. This approach first enables the organization and then leads to improvements in information, project outcomes, and ultimately business performance.

We will investigate the application of these concepts in subsequent chapters as we explore the particulars behind organizational structure and business value.

Chapter Summary

While the industry inches closer to what data governance represents it remains a very dynamic discipline today with different meanings for individual people and organizations. The evolution of this practice continues to raise the bar and visibility among the business community and for some, like this author, it is transforming itself into the broader practice of Enterprise Information Asset Management.

It is imperative to understand what people actually mean when they refer to data governance. Individuals and organizations frequently speak to one form of data governance or the other without fully understanding and/or communicating the entire picture. In many cases, it creates a confusing heap of information that CxOs, business leaders, and even subject matter experts do not completely understand. Coming to terms with what influences data and information outcomes can help an organization better recognize what needs governing. Furthermore, segmenting data governance into basic categories can bring clarity to the discipline, to the project, and draws focus where needed.

As a business defines its data governance program, it needs to be mindful of establishing a strong administrative arm to drive it. An organization's response to this exercise will determine whether the program becomes a casualty of the grassroots generation or establishes itself as a legitimate and successful data asset practice within the company.

Chapter 3

Business Benefits

Five Areas to Find Value

The industry continues to tout the value behind data governance but endures itself to the struggle of how to convince C-level leadership. Hence the reason why executive support can be hard to come by and why so many companies struggle to launch and sustain successful programs. The good news is that there is a compelling return on investment for data governance that flows directly and indirectly to the bottom line of the company. The intricacies of this discipline make it challenging but certainly not impossible to uncover the true economic affect it has on the overall business.

If the Value Exists, Why Have I Not Heard about It?

Of all the value propositions for data governance, none is more compelling than when the impact can be directly tied to an organization's business operations. This is especially true if the results can be tangibly measured and if businesses actually invest the time and effort to calculate and record the outcomes.

As a CxO or business leader, you probably ask yourself and others a very legitimate question.

"If data governance is so important why don't I hear and read more about success stories and case studies that demonstrate how it impacts a company's business outcomes?"

The truth of the matter is that most organizations that invoke governance activities seldom measure or share the impact this has on the bottom line. One reason points to a common industry practice where measuring results against a business case, goals, and objectives takes a back seat to just getting things done and moving on to the next project. Another basis is that businesses are simply reacting to what is an embarrassing situation within their company and certainly do not want to share this information publicly. Yet another widespread scenario that comes into play are the number of organizations that implement successful governance and quality initiatives but are reluctant to share it with the industry due to internal policies against it, confidentiality of the circumstances, fear that it will expose their dirty laundry, and/or they view it as a guarded competitive advantage.

During my time as a consultant, I have had the privilege to present and facilitate a number of client and prospect events. A long-standing objective at these forums has been to engage organizations in conversation with each other by having them share their information management experiences, challenges, solutions, and success stories. In one memorable client event I participated in, we had several attendees from two rival airline companies. Needless to say, silence dominated the day and made for a very awkward roundtable session. While both organizations had valuable insight neither one was willing to share it publicly due to the competitive environment that existed between them.

The reluctance of many organizations to come forward and tell their data governance story even creates a dilemma for software vendors and consultants that work in this space. The challenge for software providers and practitioners is getting clients to develop and share case studies and success stories as it pertains to the products and services they have purchased. More often than not, it is not that client organizations did not like what they were sold, rather few ever go back to chronicle the results of their acquisition and implementation, especially in business terms.

I would venture to say that less than two percent of all organizations actually attempt to measure quality and governance results against business outcomes. For the other 98 plus percent, their actions still acknowledge the value behind quality and governance solutions even though these organizations do not document it. After all, these same organizations keep renewing software maintenance fees, procure upgrades, acquire complimentarily products, and purchase additional services even though they may not take the time to quantify how vendor products and services have positively influenced business outcomes.

Due to theses long standing practices there are not as many well-documented end-to-end examples of how data governance impacts business performance as one might think. However, this is clearly a "tip of the iceberg" sort of situation. Organizations that have taken the time to measure success against business performance have a compelling story to tell. On the contrary, it should not be implied that those that do not quantify or publish business outcomes did not achieve success.

Five Primary Areas for Business Benefit for Data Governance

Finding business benefit let alone compelling value can be a daunting task for anyone in the data governance space. The key to uncovering the value of this discipline is to first look at it from a holistic perspective rather than a single project or task. Second is to recognize that while there may be short-term business benefits the greatest value comes with the maturity of the program. Third is to identify with the fact that it delivers both tangible and intangible benefits that flow directly and indirectly to the bottom line. Finally, it is to break this discipline down into manageable parts in order to understand where specific benefits reside and how they reflect in the company financial statements.

At a high level, data governance benefits can be found within five primary areas:

1) Data governance program infrastructure (Program)
2) Data management operations
3) Projects
4) Business operations
5) Organization strategy and policy

Collectively, these benefits drive value in six primary ways: financial, operational efficiencies, risk mitigation, compliance, customer/partner satisfaction, and market/competitive position. As illustrated in Figure 3.1, these benefits and their value reflect in the financial performance of the organization.

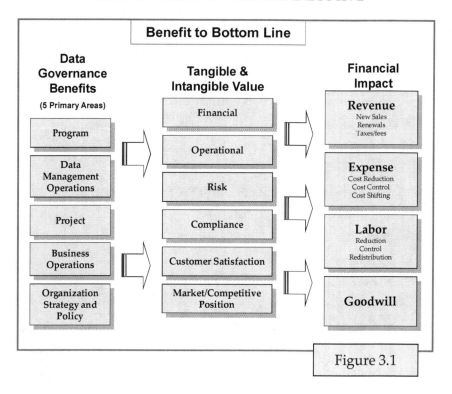

Figure 3.1

At a high level this model makes fundamental sense; however, like anything else the devil is in the details. In order to expose the actual value these benefits generate an organization must look to the particulars within each of the five primary areas of benefit. As illustrated in Figure 3.2, it is within these five categories that a wealth of opportunity exists for organizations. While the five areas of business benefit are important to note, it is the subcategories within these groups that hold the answers for business value.

It is within this collection of topics that organizations can expect to find the true value for data governance. However, the depth and breadth of each of these topics is extensive and that is why the next five chapters are dedicated to these very subject matters.

Program	Data Management	Project	Business Operations	Organization Strategy & Policy
Strategy and Direction	Data Quality	MDM	Sales and Marketing	Customer Definition
	Data Modeling	BI	Risk and Compliance	Merger and Acquisition
Structure	Metadata Management	CRM		
Scope		CDI	Customer Service	Project and Budgetary Planning
Prioritization	Data Integration	DW		
Policy	Data Lineage	EDW	Order-to-Cash	
Roles and Responsibilities	Data Security and Privacy	Data Mart	Taxes, Fees, and Payments	Technology Selection
Authority and Accountability	Data Standards	EIM	Mail and Transport	Data Enrichment
Issue Resolution	Business Rules	EPM/EPMI		Business Partner Integration
	Business Process	Search	Supply Chain	
Business Alignment	Data Stewardship	Predictive Analytics	Social and Human Services	
Power to Question	Reporting	360° View	Asset Management	
Transparency	Measure and Monitor	Data Migration	Business Analytics and Research	
Weights and Balances				
Center of Excellence				
Agility to Respond				

5 Areas of Business Benefit for Data Governance

Figure 3.2

Before we move ahead to the next chapter and explore the details behind economic justification, it is important to note a few concepts when it comes to establishing business value for this discipline.

1) True business value for data governance comes from economic and operational visibility into the entire picture, both tangible and intangible, and not the value it brings from an individual project. In fact, the more an organization scales the program across projects, data life cycles, regional, national, and international operations, the more valuable it becomes to the business.

2) Due to the complex nature of data, it is literally impossible to explore and quantify every conceivable way that data governance can drive value. In fact, it would be cost prohibitive in most organizations. However, this section and ensuing chapters should provide a good roadmap of where to look and where to dig for business value and in a way that many in the industry have found it.

3) Depending on your industry, not every area within the five categories will necessarily apply to your company, agency, or institution. Furthermore, the specific circumstances within your business will dictate the payback and whether the benefits are immediate and short or long-term in nature.

4) It is advisable that every organization conduct a business case, and not just a superficial one, even if the benefits are self-evident. Aside from securing funding, it should be used to educate the masses as to the purpose and value for the program, provide a basis for measuring performance, and help protect it from perpetual corporate reorganization going forward.

Chapter Summary

The business value for data governance may have been elusive for organizations in the past but that is not to say it has not been there all along. Breaking it down into manageable parts, venturing outside the data management domain, and taking a holistic versus project-based approach to finding value is the difference between a feeble and compelling business case.

At the end of the day, it is all about demonstrating value and the next several chapters will help you come to appreciate the finer points of this discipline and the value it brings to organizations of all size and complexity.

Chapter 4

Program Value

Program value represents the intrinsic value that comes from simply implementing a data governance body to lead, manage, and govern corporate data and information assets. Many program layer benefits are intangible in the beginning but become real as hidden opportunities are exposed and risk mitigated. There is also a case to be made for the value the program brings in positioning the company to accomplish things that would otherwise be unachievable.

Strategy/Direction/Structure/ Scope/Prioritization

A data governance program yields immediate value to the organization from the standpoint that it provides the framework for organizing and managing an entity's information assets. By providing strategy, structure, and direction alone, it sets in motion the company's ability to gather information, make cross-functional decisions, set priorities, respond to crisis and opportunity, and take actions that are clearly improbable for most organizations today.

In the absence of data governance how does an organization expect to effectively accomplish this?

Authority/Accountability//Roles/Resp onsibilities/Policy/Issue Resolution

A key aspect to data governance is how it organizes people, process, and technologies by defining who is responsible for what, when, and how – and holding everyone accountable. This is a prerequisite for any company that is serious about solving their information asset management problems.

As noted throughout this book, the presence or absence of authority and accountability is the difference between a successful or unsuccessful data governance initiative. A formal data governance program equipped with the necessary authority will drive benefit through its ability to organize the masses, develop policy, resolve issues, and hold people accountable. In other words, exactly what you want this program to accomplish!

In the absence of a data governance program, how else does a company plan to hold people accountable and achieve the desired results?

Business Alignment

One of the biggest barriers to effectively managing data assets is the culture and politics often associated with various lines of business. Getting everyone to play nice in the sandbox is possibly the biggest obstacle to success. Moreover, attempting to accomplish this on a voluntary or near voluntary basis is a ridiculous thought when it comes to governance.

It takes a formal process to align business units around a common data management strategy. Data governance is the mechanism and change agent to navigate these obstacles.

Power to Question

Organizations are filled with territorial self-interests where people are offended and more than mildly suspicious if you ask to examine their data, business processes, and data practices. This environment further fragments the data life cycle and thwarts the organization from understanding and solving data related problems. Under the umbrella of the data governance program the organization should have the power to question data management practices and outcomes that would almost certainly go unchallenged today.

I have personally witnessed a number of situations where a well-founded quality or governance initiative comes to a complete halt because of the lack of cooperation by a single individual or business unit. In each instance, the individuals spearheading the campaign had no power to critically question or engage the parties that were creating the road blocks. The unfortunate thing is that I have seen this scenario play out more times than you can ever imagine. The benefit of enabling the power to question is in exposing opportunities and risk that would otherwise remain hidden to the organization.

Transparency

This is possibly the greatest benefit of a data governance initiative. We are reminded everyday about the need for transparency in private and public sectors. Whether mandated or not, most everyone agrees that it probably a good thing. Unfortunately, most organizations don't know how to go about creating a lucid culture nor do they always understand the value of it. Data governance introduces a business process that is known to proactively create transparency and deliver a number of benefits from it.

A well-formed and well-represented data governance program drives transparency by the very nature of its being. It brings together business and IT and a meeting of the right minds that simply does not exist in your company today. In doing so, it uncovers unthinkable opportunities and risk across the board. Additionally, this process elevates the level of education and decision making within the company.

In all my dealings with organizations my favorite time is when people from diverse backgrounds come together in the same room for the first time or even the second or third. The interaction that takes place never ceases to amaze me and the opportunities that flow from it are astounding.

A few years ago, I was working with a Fortune 500 company that had decided to implement a data governance program for a number of good reasons. My role was to assist the company in building the framework for the program. Part of this engagement involved the creation and implementation of a data governance council. Five or six of the company's vice presidents (VP) attended the first council meeting. In a few cases, this was the first that these individuals had met. One VP had lobbied to be on the council in order to resolve a long-standing data problem that had created large amounts of manual work for their department. When the issue was raised during the meeting another VP turned to the inquiring party and said "consider it done." Resolving the issue was not the problem, getting the right people in the room under the right circumstances was the challenge. As a result, the VP that had his problem solved was able to reduce head count and shift a full time resource to another part of his operations where it was needed.

Another transparency example I witnessed is how data governance helped a financial institution bring visibility to lost sales within two of their business units. Because of the latency of information across global markets, two business units were struggling with operational delays in getting the global credit information they need to complete sales and minimize overall risk to the company. The business knew they were losing sales that they could not close the same day and that the company was exposed to unnecessary risk whenever they completed sales without having the full credit information they needed. Neither business group was aware that the other was having a similar problem and both had concluded that this was simply how the process worked. IT was not aware of the business problem at all.

Through a data governance initiative the two lines of business and IT happened to end up in the same room together where the topic was raised inadvertently. Once all the parties understood the problem a relatively straightforward solution was devised via a combination of business process and technology. The results from the solution were expected to recover a minimum of $200,000 in lost sales revenues per year and reduce overall exposure to the company by nearly $3,000,000. This would NEVER have happened under a business as usual arrangement.

Another example that I will expand upon later in this book is how a team of IT folks came together to fix their customer data problems, specifically around address information. As part of this process I requested that they include the business in our meetings as well as supply a data flow diagram that we could walk through. The IT folks were apprehensive in asking the business to participate because they felt it was an IT issue. The other reason is that they really did not know who in the business should participate because they hardly knew anyone in the business.

The governance process brought transparency to the magnitude of the problem from both an IT and business perspective. IT was focusing on trying to fix a single data source when in fact there were ten others that required fixing in order to resolve the problem completely. The lone businessperson that attended the meeting noted that there were nine people dedicated full-time to working with return mail, a fact that was completely unknown to IT. The governance process not only expanded IT's view of the problem and solution but also provided them the business case to fund the project!

The number of unknown opportunities is countless and cannot be ignored. Whether governance exposes redundancy and rework or revenue and risk, the discoveries are astounding. In support of this, I always recommend that data governance organizations maintain a transparency log to record all the anonymous opportunities that are uncovered by this very process and are likely to never have been known to the company otherwise. Companies simply don't know what they don't know until a compelling event takes place or visibility is created within the company.

In the absence of data governance what is your organization doing to create visibility into your data and information assets? Are you waiting for that compelling event or do you want to take a proactive approach and try to head it off before it happens? Can I always tell you exactly what the impact will be to the bottom line, where and when it will show up? No. Is there value in creating transparency around information assets? Absolutely!

Weights and Balances

I have run across far too many situations where the power and control of data and information assets resides in a single camp if not a single person. The result of this unbalanced power creates significant problems within an organization, most notable being that it costs the company a lot of money. A well-formulated data governance program balances power and positions the company to make more informed, better, and less self-serving decisions going forward.

A few years back I was working with a very large technology firm that was implementing technology and data management processes to more than 20 countries worldwide. I was responsible for assisting the company with developing overall strategy and an implementation plan. Prior to my first on-site meeting I had recommended that we invite a number of business and IT stakeholders to the initial planning session since each of them would be instrumental in the success of the project. When I arrived I was met by two people from IT - that was it. When I asked where the business was they responded, "the business will just screw it up." I spent a good portion of the next nine hours, in a very tiny conference room, trying to convince these IT folks to rethink their position.

Unfortunately, I failed in my attempts and spent a fair amount of time instead placing disclaimers on my services. Three months and over $150,000 in project costs later, the IT folks came back to me requesting that we engage the business and revise the project plan accordingly. The cost to the company and the hit to the professional reputations of the IT folks were significant. Regrettably the company never realized what happened or never felt compelled to take action.

A company recently asked me to conduct a data governance and data quality workshop for their organization. The person spearheading the workshop wanted to expand the thinking within the company around data governance. As part of any activity of this nature, I made sure that there was an appropriate mix of business and IT professionals invited to the event. One week before the workshop I received a call from one of the co-stakeholders that informed me that I could not mention anything about data governance and the workshop should only cover quality. The request was clearly an effort to protect political interests though I never fully understood the reason until I was in the meeting.

The workshop was attended only by IT employees; no business people. One domineering individual, employed by the company for 30 years, a data architect by trade, and the resident expert on data governance, dominated all conversation on the client side. In fact the co-stakeholder that counseled me a week earlier never said a word all day. Neither did a few other people. It became immediately obvious that everyone in the room was afraid to challenge this person and that this individual alone called the shots around data management. This was a very unfortunate situation because the primary problems they were having with a global data quality deployment were directly attributed to their inability to execute at the governance layer. All of which pointed to a person with too much power and a very limited view of the world.

One of my most unusual experiences came from a government agency. The organization hired an IT Director that was given carte blanche to do as they pleased. This individual took it upon himself to determine who had access to what data; removed disk and flash drive capabilities from computers, and required business people to go to a public computer and printer to copy or print documents, including sensitive information. Consequently, the business was effectively crippled from performing routine work. To top it off, this person dressed in black every day including a full-length trench coat that he wore through the halls of the agency on a daily basis. Wow!

Now, this person was hired and reported directly to the head of the agency that happened to be ignorant on the topic of technology...and probably a few other things. It is needless to say both management and staff were up in arms with the entire situation. Ultimately, this person was fired over questionable financial activities leaving a wake of destruction in their path. The good news is the agency recovered but not without spending significant amounts of time and money undoing the damage. The bad news is the head of the agency is still there.

Now you may be sitting there thinking that could never happen in your company and I am here to attest to the fact that this occurs far more often than you think. These are not isolated incidences by any means. A strong data governance program mitigates these types of behaviors and eradicates them if they already exist. Like a good democracy, it provides weights and balances for the benefit of all and especially for the organization itself.

Center of Excellence (CoE) or Competency Center

A data governance framework provides organizations the flexibility to create a Center of Excellence or competency center in order to capture and cultivate specialized skills and processes that can be leveraged across multiple projects. In the absence of a center of excellence, organizations find that their proficiency wanes as they duplicate and recreate skills and activities on a project-by-project basis. In addition, it propagates the dreaded silo environment. Most importantly, it drives costs up in a number of ways.

- Education and training (applications, technologies, business process, domain)
- Rework and redundancy
- Extended implementation time frames

- Increased project risks
- Lost opportunities
- Lowers return on investment (ROI)

Growing a Center of Excellence helps centralize elusive intellectual property and offset the intellectual fragmentation that goes with historical silo practices. This competency center often applies to domains such as data quality, data modeling, reporting, stewardship, project management, and other cross-functional data intensive activities. It also helps institutionalize best practice methodologies, standards, and processes that are essential to keeping costs down and business performance up.

Agility to Respond

The data governance framework allows a company to better respond to random crisis, indiscriminate decision support, and urgent business matters that have dependencies on company data for resolution. In addition, it provides the infrastructure for the company to learn from the event and put safeguards in place for dealing with similar situations going forward.

The agility to respond goes well beyond those moments of crisis and pushes down to the day-to-day operations. Governance gives the organization dexterity to respond to everyday data management challenges that can head off those high profile predicaments that are all too familiar.

Every organization has a story about an informational crisis of some sort that could have been avoided, minimized, or addressed more quickly. In many cases these situations cost the company significant amounts of money, time, and resources to resolve. In the absence of a formal process or authority to turn to, these events often leave the organization in the same vulnerable position it was when the crisis began.

Data governance provides the agility an organization needs to understand and respond to their data and informational requirements more effectively. In addition, to institute processes and best practices to prevent such events from happening again.

Chapter Summary

The program layer of benefits for data governance is about enabling an organization to do things that cannot be accomplished in a business as usual environment. First are the benefits that flow from establishing an infrastructure that can begin to manage the data and information asset environment centrally. Secondly, it is about the capabilities that are unleashed as a result of putting the infrastructure in place.

My question to you: in the absence of a formal data governance program, how do you intend to effectively coordinate, manage, and derive the most business value from the data and information assets within your organization?

Chapter 5

Data Management Operations Value

The value data governance brings to data management operations is derived from orchestrating data management functions and activities between the business, IT, and across lines of business. Much of the worth in this category comes from operational improvements, efficiencies, and enabling these functions to flourish across a data life cycle or enterprise. Benefits typically point to cost reduction, cost avoidance, labor reduction, and labor redistribution. These operational efficiencies also make it possible to optimize business performance associated with business operations and projects, which I will cover in subsequent chapters.

For each section in this chapter, I have included a set of sample of questions that you as the executive or business sponsor may want

---

to consider asking your business and technical leadership in order to kick start discussions within these areas of focus. While these questions may be useful for initiating talks, I have always found them to be even more valuable when you ask them in front of a mixed technical and business audience rather than in a one-on-one setting. When it comes to data governance, getting to the bottom of things is best accomplished in mixed company.

Data Quality

The industry embraces several explanations for data quality. Essentially, it is the practice of ensuring data is accurate, complete, consistent, reliable, valid, timely, and trustworthy for the intended use by the business and it involves activities such as profiling, cleansing, standardizing, and matching data. Data quality is arguably the most influential data management function for steering data outcomes and the overall success of any data intensive project. It could also be said that the purpose of every project is to supply quality information to the business, which further corroborates the importance of this discipline within an organization.

Historically data quality has been viewed as a technology solution for automating data hygiene across large data sets and high volume environments. While state-of-the-art technology plays mission critical roles in any data quality program it is not the only factor that determines quality outcomes. At its core it goes back to the old saying "garbage in, garbage out," which remains remarkably accurate today given that technology can only do so much to correct bad information.

The challenge with data quality is that it has several dependencies, most notably being people, processes, and technology that collectively influence the condition of the data. Further complicating the picture, these dependencies are often embedded in upstream and downstream processes and fall out of reach and/or out of sight of core project objectives and budgets. As a result, companies spend millions of dollars on the latest and greatest technologies but fail to address the cross-functional business processes and other quality issues that quickly erode their return on investment and lead to unfulfilled expectations. The industry is full of examples that reflect failure around CRM, MDM, DW, BI, EDW, CDI and other major projects because the company underestimated, or simply ignored, the need to address the data quality life cycle.

While more and more organizations are attending to quality related initiatives, the reality is that most are barely scratching the surface. Of those that have implemented data quality most have done so within a single project and normally within a single technology alone. Few actually tackle the full data life cycle, let alone address multiple data domains or enterprise initiatives, leaving ample opportunity to improve revenues and reduce costs.

Countless surveys and case studies have been conducted through the years that indicate organizations are losing millions of dollars annually due to poor data quality. Returning our attention to the The Gartner (2009) survey suggests that, on average organizations lose $8.2 million dollars a year due to data quality issues. Forbes Insights (2010) reports that companies lose about $5 million dollars due to data related problems. Gartner goes on to report that 22 percent estimate that they lose $20 million dollars per year while Forbes Insights reports that 20 percent of their respondents also estimated a $20 million dollar per year loss.

Both of these surveys underscore what many of us have suspected or known for some time. While it is difficult to quantify losses precisely, there is no doubt that data quality has a significant impact on business performance. We will explore the details on how data quality affects business operations in Chapter 7. In the meantime this chapter focuses on how data governance influences the data quality practice within data management operations.

Data governance is the instrument that enables organizations to implement data quality practices across the entire data life cycle as well as the enterprise. This optimizes data management and business operations in a number of ways.

- Enables data quality to expand from a single project or technology-based solution to a full data life cycle and/or enterprise level discipline.

- Permits organizations to address data quality strategies within the various upstream and downstream business processes that impact overall data outcomes.

- Provides a mechanism to incorporate comprehensive data quality strategies into every data centric project going forward and as far upstream as the planning and budgeting process.

- Provides the framework for business and technology professionals to collaborate on the development, implementation, and reporting of quality standards.

- Improves data outcomes for a broader range of projects (CRM, BI, MDM, etc.) and business operations.

- Exposes and addresses the timeliness of data and information that are commonly overlooked by traditional data quality practices.

- Provides a forum for making more informed, and more balanced data quality decisions when it comes to technology, implementation, data enrichment, organization policy, and other information quality sensitive decisions.

- Allows for the specialization of a specialty discipline.

Another very interesting benefit of data governance is how it raises the awareness of data quality and therefore increases the trust the company has in its own data. Organizations that are aware of how data quality works and how it is managed in their own organization are much more likely to trust the data than those companies that have no visibility into the data quality practices of their company. In turn, this trust or lack of trust can have a profound affect on the decisions companies make around their data and whether they are based largely on facts or false perceptions.

As an executive you should consider asking the following of your data management leadership.

1) What do we do today to address data quality? Does it address the entire data life cycle or is it a spot solution?
2) To what extent does our data quality practice address business process and technology?
3) Is data quality a component of every data intensive project we launch? If so, to what extent? If not, why not?
4) In your opinion where is data quality working and not working?
5) What is the impact to the business? Do we even know?
6) Have we ever conducted a formal data audit or assessment to actually measure the condition of our data and how it impacts the business?
7) In your opinion what needs to be done to address any data quality shortcomings that may exist? Should this be addressed with technology? Business process redesign? Or both?

Data Modeling

A data model represents how data is organized within company applications and databases. The data model plays a very important role in defining how data gets into applications, how data is retrieved, understanding and maintaining referential relationships with other data, and determining how data integrates to other applications. Data modeling is an IT responsibility and represents the practice, process, and methodologies used to create and maintain a data model.

Many of the early concepts and calls for data governance began with the data modeling community. Much of this was driven from the explosion of open source systems, merger and acquisition that has shaped the fragmented data environment we know today. This complex situation heightened the need to coordinate common data models across different development teams and applications in order to ensure quality, accelerate development time, reduce costs, and make data more accessible to the business.

A simplistic example of a complex data model situation is where an organization stores similar customer data in five different databases in the following fashion.

> Customer ID: The customer identification field exists in only three of the five systems. The database field name differs for each (CustID, ID, CID). One is numeric, one is alphabetic, and one is alpha numeric and all have a different allowed field length. In addition, the formatting of the customer ID in two systems is non-standard.

> Address: Customer addresses exist in all five systems. One system stores the address in a single field but truncates the data due to a limited field length. Another system allows for the storage of discrete address components (street name, PO Box, Suite, City, State, Postal Code) but only

allows for address line one. Two systems allow for storing discrete address components but cannot adequately support international addresses so data is commonly populated in incorrect fields. One system places all address data into address line one and line two. The naming conventions for all data elements differ between systems as does the field length. Data quality and address standardization reside in one system.

As you can see from this simplistic example, the complexity of a data model can grow exponentially as organizations add systems and incorporate more data domains and data elements. With this complexity comes an increase in cost to implement and maintain data dependent projects. In addition, the more intricate a data model the more constrained it becomes in defining data relationships and delivering the data and information a business requires.

Unfortunately, many organizations do not have a common data model. In reality it may be unattainable for many businesses to adopt and implement. At minimum organizations need to work toward optimizing what they do have. This includes doing what many organizations have yet to do and that is to document their model. Aside from the fragmented data environment, there are two very pronounced reasons for this. The first comes from the age-old practice of "just get it done" with no regard or consideration given to long-term implications of shortsighted decisions. The other is the absence of data governance where modelers have struggled with adopting and maintaining standards across people, work groups, systems, and projects.

The excessive costs for supporting a multifaceted/non-standard data model are due to increased complexity, redundancy and rework on a number of fronts. There are various industry estimates on this but many fall in line with what people have shared with me; and that is the notion that 20-40 percent of the time and cost associated with activities such as developing interfaces, building data warehouses and data marts are attributed to redundancy and rework. Keep in mind that interface costs can represent 20-70 percent of the cost of an application. This is all very interesting to me because I know of an organization that has over 250 data marts, all without metadata and they keep adding on. Ouch!

Data governance can help the data modeling community develop and implement standards, mobilize subject matter expertise, and create documentation for work groups and projects; all of which drive down development costs and create a more agile data environment.

As an executive you should consider asking the following questions of your chief data modeler.

1) In your opinion how manageable, unmanageable, and agile is our data model?
2) How does the current model constrain your group's ability to service business requirements?
3) In your opinion how much redundancy and rework do you believe exists today due to our data model?
4) If we had a solid data governance program would it help you standardize and improve upon the data model and

reduce the redundancy and rework? If so, by how much? How else might a strong data governance program help you?

Metadata Management

Yes, metadata is data about the data; but more importantly, it is the high level practice of documenting the data and the data environment within a company. Having documentation handy whenever companies are planning and building for a data warehouse, data mart, CRM, application interface, report and any number of other data related projects can be extremely useful. It cuts down on the time and cost associated with planning, development, testing and completing the task. In addition, it improves the quality of the final results.

Like any other business function, documentation lends itself to smoother operations. Take, for example, an organization that was moving from a legacy mainframe system to a new open source application to mange core parts of their business. Part of the migration effort was to deal with recreating legacy reports in the new system. The company discovered that they were generating over 4,000 reports every day in the legacy system and very few of them had any metadata associated with them (business owner, date created, purpose, calculations, where data came from, etc.). Keep in mind that many of these reports were created several years prior by people who were no longer with the company.

The first question the company had to face was, "do we really need all of these reports?" The answer was "probably not" but that led to the next set of questions of "where do we go to find out," and "who do we talk to?" The company eventually determined which reports were necessary and which ones were not, but not before spending significant amounts of time and money understanding the problem and then developing the new reports. In this case, had the organization maintained metadata on their reports it would have saved them hundreds of thousands of dollars on this project alone.

As in the previous example, report metadata seems to be a sore spot for many organizations. Various companies with whom I have worked share common war stories about generating reports, especially non-standard ones. The story normally follows a path where it took weeks to create the report and another several weeks or months to reconcile it. In many cases, the metadata deficiencies were a principal culprit. Metadata clearly affects the cost, timeliness, and quality of decision support information.

While the direct cost of not having metadata is not always visible, the costs can be far reaching. Take for example the company I mentioned earlier that has more than 250 data marts and little to no metadata associated with them. The company also has experienced a fair amount of turnover through the years along with a number of quality problems. I do not have visibility into what this company paid out through the years when it comes to time and expense associated with rework, redundancy, maintenance, training, and explaining these data marts. A reasonable guesstimate is that these costs have reached into the tens of millions of dollars, much of what could have been avoided or significantly reduced with documented metadata.

Data governance helps expose metadata problems and formulate comprehensive strategies to overcome them.

As an executive you should consider asking the following of your data management leadership.

1) In your opinion what is the state of our metadata management across the company?
2) In your opinion what areas of the business are most vulnerable due to the lack of metadata?
3) In your opinion what is the impact our metadata situation has on operations and the business?
4) In your opinion what needs to be done to reverse the situation?

Data Integration

Data integration is a very fundamental aspect of data management because it is the basis for connecting, accessing, and moving data between heterogeneous sources. In simplistic technical jargon, this is how organizations "hard wire" data together so that common information can be shared and accessed from a central location or virtual databases via queries, search engines, and other user interfaces. There are a number of different data integration models, methods, and technologies embraced by IT professionals. These practices and solutions incorporate a number of tools and functions and can consist of a network of real time, near real time, batch, and trickle feed data strategies. Needless to say this sort of stuff tugs at the heart strings of the technologist but, depending on your point of view, either underwhelms or overwhelms the business community. This begs the question, "why does the business need to be involved in data integration and where does governance fit into the equation?"

While the data integration discipline remains tech-heavy, it still has room for business and governance involvement. There are four primary reasons for this. One is so the business can collaborate with IT and develop the required data policies to be implemented within the integrated solutions. The second is to leverage the data governance arm to drive standards, consistency, and reusability across technical teams and integration initiatives. The third is to help the business clearly understand the opportunities, options, risk, and constraints of data integration and how it will affect business outcomes. The fourth is to guard against the status quo where technology teams can fall into the pattern of only proposing what they are comfortable with delivering or want to deliver based on their skills, tools, and resources.

Just to put this in perspective, what was the cost of your last data warehouse project? Was it seven figures as many are? Did the results meet your expectations? How many data integration projects has your company had to redesign or scrap entirely because it did not meet expectations? Also, what is the cost to the organization for using non-standard tools and practices when developing and implementing data integration projects? Since most organizations operate in a silo environment they frequently face excessive operational costs associated with a large inventory of integration tools. The silo approach also dilutes intellectual property which extends project timelines and drives up the cost of projects, education, training, and maintenance.

Data governance ensures that business and IT are more tightly coupled in the data integration decision-making process. It ensures business requirements and data policy are clearly expressed during the planning stage and, in turn, that technologists clearly explain to the business the various concepts, options, risks, and constraints for each technical approach. It also is central for orchestrating the activities of independent data integration work groups and projects that may exist across the enterprise which help contain costs associated with future investment and solution maintenance.

The governance process alone leads to better data integration solutions. It reduces the cost of reworking integration projects, shortens project life cycles, reduces the overall investment in integration tools, and strengthens intellectual capital. Perhaps most important is that it helps educate the business and sets common expectations across the enterprise. Many of these operational efficiencies cannot be tangibly measured. However, it is reasonable to assume, based on historical practices and industry experiences that hidden cost reductions would kick in over time by elevating the presence of data governance for data integration.

As an executive, you should consider asking the following questions of your business stakeholders and data integration technology leads.

1) Does our current data integration strategy (data warehouse, data mart, data virtualization, etc.) satisfy the requirements of the business? If not, why not?

2) How much involvement did the business have in the current data integration architecture? Explain.

3) What are the greatest inefficiencies associated with our current data integration architecture? What is it costing the organization?

4) Are there more advanced technologies and approaches that we should consider in order to improve our data integration capabilities and business performance? Explain.

5) In your estimation, what steps should the organization begin to take to optimize our data integration capabilities and why?

Data Lineage

Data lineage is the area of data management that tracks data from the point of origination through every subsequent transaction and event going forward. This provides the business with the ability to effectively view, report, and audit the historical life cycle of the information. Some may suggest that this is part of metadata management from a data integration perspective. In concept yes;

however, the specialization of this practice and the profound impact it has on certain industries cannot be emphasized enough.

In many respects data lineage is heavily compliance driven. In the financial sector, it supports Basel Accords and other requirements for financial institutions. In the pharmaceutical industry, it is about tracking clinical trials. Healthcare providers and researchers depend on data lineage to track the receipt, transfer, issuance, validation, implant, and disposal of an implant or tissue. Airlines depend on it to track maintenance and parts for aircraft. For some research firms, lineage is about historical tracking and trending the price of precious metals or commodities against historical events in order to predict forthcoming market conditions and outcomes.

The business case for data lineage is covers a number of areas. Many of which cannot be fully quantified until the problem actually surfaces. However, all of which make sound business sense.

- What is the value of being able to accurately trend data and events within an organization or industry? In order to do so, a business must have the capacity to store and access historical data that relate to these events.

- What is the risk and subsequent cost to the organization if it is found to be non-compliant? What are the potential costs from regulatory fines, legal fees, responding to a public relations calamity, the hit to company reputation, and lost future business?

- Companies that have efficient data lineage in place will lower their internal and external auditing costs. Auditors will spend less time conducting and verifying an audit if the information is readily available, well organized, and it appears accurate.

- Data lineage has much of the same value proposition as metadata management and data modeling in the sense that it reduces the redundancy and rework associated with the development, testing, and implementation of data integration and reporting projects.

Data governance provides the framework to oversee and coordinate data lineage activities and solutions in a way that support compliance, reduce risk, and accentuate opportunities for the organization.

As an executive you should consider asking the following of your chief data architect and business leadership.

1) Given our industry what dependencies do we have on data lineage?
2) In your opinion what is the state of our data lineage across the company?
3) In your opinion what areas in both the business and IT sectors of the company are most vulnerable due to insufficient data lineage and why?
4) In your opinion what should the company be doing to correct the situation?

Security & Privacy

The livelihood of your organization depends on having data and information assets safeguarded against disaster, loss, theft, and fraudulent activities. While physical security of databases and servers has become a routine practice, with all the state-of-the-art disaster recovery, data storage, and fail over systems in place, there are a number of potential security and privacy risks that remain inside and outside of core systems. Most of these security challenges come from various areas of the business. Data governance provides the opportunity for uncovering and addressing these unique cross-functional challenges in order to mitigate the threats and advance the opportunities.

The following are examples of security and privacy risks that can be effectively addressed by a well-formed data governance body.

- Data access - Access privileges are often determined and set by IT which may be too restrictive for certain areas of the business to conduct their work. As a result, productivity is compromised and opportunities missed. On the other hand, if access is disproportionately influenced by business functions, the company may be exposed to more risk than it should absorb. Can you say WikiLeaks? Data governance brings visibility and balance to this process.

- Spreadsheets – This is a great desktop tool but a potentially dangerous one as well. Downloading information into spreadsheets and onto laptops places the company at risk of exposing confidential information either accidentally or maliciously. While spreadsheets are not expected to go away anytime soon, data governance can help the organization gain visibility into the problem and work towards implementing practical, risk-mitigating solutions that minimize spreadsheet use and maximize their purpose.

- Desktop databases (Access, etc.) – Like spreadsheets, these applications are very useful but introduce a new level of risk into the organization.

- Media – The explosion of information, where, and how we share it creates a whole new set of challenges for today's businesses. Data is easily and instantaneously shared within and outside the company via e-mail, flash memory, CD-ROM, external hard drives and other media. While this does wonders for day-to-day business, it has taken security and privacy concerns to an entirely new level.

- Other files and information – Today we exchange data and information in e-mail, text files, word documents, portable document format (PDF), presentations such as PowerPoint, and digital images (.jpg, .bmp, etc.). Much of what is shared is confidential, legally binding, and even regulated. A data governance body is positioned to gradually expand their scope into this area of data and information security.

As you can see, there are multiple ways that security and privacy can be compromised with debilitating consequences on the business. One example I often share with people relates to a company that had over 30,000 spreadsheets with many stored on public domain servers and laptops within the organization. Of these spreadsheets, at least ten were being used to support daily business transactions outside of core systems. To compound the problem the business had thousands of image files and other sensitive documents that were stored on public domains, desktops, and laptops. Collectively, the security and privacy risk to the company was determined to be extensive.

The data governance group that exposed the spreadsheet security risk stepped in to address the challenge. The team's objective was not to rid the company of their reliance on spreadsheets. It was to ensure that spreadsheets, especially those with the most sensitive information were secure and accessible to only those individuals that actually needed them. The group also focused on minimizing the reliance on spreadsheets for day-to-day transaction processing and tightened up business processes that surrounded all these activities.

A data governance discipline is the eyes and ears of the organization when it comes to monitoring and managing the integrity and security of data and information. As our data universe becomes more distributed and complex, there is no better avenue for identifying security risks and ensuring privacy than through a well-formed data governance group.

As an executive you should consider asking the following questions of your IT and business leadership.

1) What are our corporate policies and practices for dealing with data security and privacy inside and outside our core systems?
2) How effective are these policies and practices working? Do we even know? If not, why not?
3) Have we quantified the challenge by completing an audit of the file types that are stored on our servers, desktops, and laptops?
4) Do you know of any files that are being used to transact critical business functions that are not a part of our core systems?
5) In your opinion what are our biggest risks and what do we need to do to mitigate them?

Data Standards

Data standards define how data is structured, as well as address aspects of data content including naming conventions, format, entity definitions, and other attributes. The more an organization can develop and implement common data standards across systems the more usable the data and the more valuable it becomes to the business. The absence or inconsistent application of data standards plays havoc in any organization and is arguably the most fundamental data management problem with far reaching consequences if not managed appropriately.

Take, for example, the organization that wants to achieve a 360-degree or unified view of their business. Depending on the nature of the business this may involve a holistic view of customers, members, prospects, business partners, materials, parts, and associated transactions and events. Achieving a unified view enables organizations to improve several business activities. However, as many companies have learned, arriving at this goal often proves difficult.

So why is this elusive? A 360-degree model involves several complex data relationships that are highly dependent on data standards to link these associations. Inconsistent data standards makes it difficult, if not impossible, to portray a single view of the information. Organizations with unreliable points of reference to their data are unable to link common records let alone represent the information accurately.

The lack of data standards also contributes to the dreaded problem of record duplication, which is probably the most undesirable data challenge a company can have. Duplication of records not only hampers business outcomes but the time and cost of identifying, consolidating, and managing a duplicate record environment is extensive.

Data standards also serve as the measuring stick for data quality. If companies do not establish data standards then there is no way they can effectively measure quality because there is no benchmark for which to evaluate it. Nor can a company begin to understand the extent of their data problems and the opportunities that it presents.

I once participated in a data audit for a well-known technology company. The organization was initially reluctant to go through the data audit/assessment process because they thought their data was in pretty good shape. As a normal course of business, we asked the organization to determine which data elements were mission critical to their business outcomes as well as provide the data standards and rules that applied to the data. The company went through a considerable struggle internally trying to determine what the standards and rules were and eventually gave us a list of what they thought the data standards should be. In other words, the organization had few defined standards and even fewer, if any, had been implemented consistently. The data audit revealed that 49 percent of their data did not meet the standards they set forth. While a financial impact analysis was never completed, the extent this problem caused the business was assumed by all parties to be in the hundreds of thousands of dollars.

Data governance drives data standards in four specific ways. First, it gets the business involved in establishing and managing corporate standards with interactive collaboration of IT. Second, it enforces the application of the standards across lines of business and technologies, which most companies clearly fall short of. Third, it ensures the standards are well-documented (metadata) and communicated within the organization. Finally, it lays the groundwork to monitor and measure data standards.

As an executive you should consider asking the following questions of your data leads and business analysts.

1) Do we have corporate level data standards in place today? If not, why not? If so, to what extent?

2) Are the data standards we have in place enforced within all the business processes and technologies they need to be? If not, why not?

3) What type of problems is the organization experiencing due to inadequate data standards?

4) How much does the business engage in developing and managing data standards?

5) Have we ever measured how well our data standards are being applied to our data? If not, why?

6) In your opinion what should the company be doing to correct any deficiencies in this area?

Business Rules

Business rules pertain to business decision logic and how it is applied to company data. Such logic commonly includes if, then, else reasoning as it relates to where, when, and how data is added, changed, merged, aggregated, coded, and/or presented to the business. Inconsistent, incomplete, incorrect, and/or undocumented business rules are certain to disrupt data outcomes and business results.

A very common example of this is how companies spend significant time and resources trying to analyze and reconcile reports. An insurance company recently shared with me how it took them several months, yes months, to reconcile three reports that IT was asked to create by senior management. The information from the reports came from multiple systems that had different business rules for the same information. In this instance, the logic for determining various codes were either different between systems or the code was derived from information that was created based on inconsistent business rules. To compound the problem, most business rules were undocumented (metadata) so technologists had to examine code in order to understand the logic.

The cost of this exercise alone was estimated to be more than $50,000 not to mention the productivity loss and the opportunity cost incurred by the business since they did not have the information they needed. Unfortunately, this type of event is hardly rare in the business world. Organizations are either spending material sums of money analyzing and reconciling data or using bad information in their business decisions because of incorrect or inconsistent business rules within their data environment.

Data governance has three primary purposes when it comes to business rules. The first is to get the business involved in establishing and managing the rules with interactive collaboration of IT. The second is to enforce and oversee the implementation of the business rules across lines of business and technologies. The third is to ensure the business rules are well-documented (metadata) and communicated within the organization.

As an executive you should consider asking the following questions of your data leads and technologists.

1) In your opinion how consistent or inconsistent are business rules applied within our various systems?
2) What type of problems is the company experiencing from inconsistent or inaccurate business rules?
3) How active is the business in developing and maintaining business rules?
4) Are business rules well documented?
5) In your opinion what should the company be doing to correct any deficiencies in this area?

Business Process

Business process pertains to the various business procedures and practices that impact data and information outcomes and normally those activities involving manual decision points and intervention. For example, when entering a new customer record into the system, should an account representative check for an existing account first or just proceed by entering a new account to save time? When entering the new account information should the representative enter a first name or will a first initial suffice? Is a valid phone number necessary or can the representative simply record the most basic requirement by entering a properly formatted yet non-valid number such as 999-9999? The technology may allow for any one or all of these scenarios so the business process must be defined and managed just as closely as the technology.

As you can see from the example above, routine actions can have a rippling effect on the usability of the data later. In this scenario, these types of data entry problems can make it very difficult to support other business processes down the line. This is especially true when it involves reconciling reports, driving marketing campaigns, and providing top-notch customer service.

Further complicating the issue, business processes are typically owned by the business unit that handles the information or transaction. This creates a situation where the process satisfies the needs of the business unit but without consideration for the data dependencies of the rest of the organization. Data governance provides the mechanism to rectify this situation and bring continuity across business processes in a way that benefits the overall organization as well as individual business operations.

As an executive you should consider asking the following questions of your data leads, business users, and technologists.

1) In your opinion how much is business process contributing to poor data outcomes? Do we really know?

2) What type of problems is the company experiencing from bad or inconsistent business processes?

3) Are the organization's business processes well documented?

4) How interactive is the business and IT in developing and maintaining business processes?

5) In your opinion what should the company be doing to correct any deficiencies in this area?

Data Stewardship

Data stewardship represents the formal organization of people, process, and technologies necessary to monitor, measure, audit, trend, report, and respond to data outcomes and anomalies on a daily and somewhat tactical basis. Stewards are essentially the eyes, ears, and custodians of the data and are commonly made up of people from cross-functional roles that include subject matter experts, analysts, database administrators (DBA), data entry clerks, and others that may touch and interact with the data on a routine basis. This group is normally the first to detect problems, opportunities, and risk at the data layer and take the appropriate actions to report and fix the data anomalies.

The principal value of a data stewardship program is that it allows an organization to take a proactive position with respect to monitoring, measuring, and responding to data issues. By keeping ahead of the game, companies can identify issues before they become a costly problem for the business and with many of these activities completed during the normal course of business at minimal cost.

Collectively, this team of people must work in unison to ensure standards, processes, and rules are applied consistently to the data and across multiple business functions. Because this requires a close formal alliance to be successful, data stewardship is a natural fit for implementing within the framework of a data governance program.

One misstep I often see organizations take is to implement a data stewardship program without any formal governance or oversight in place. The expectation under this scenario is that people will cooperate and do the right thing to manage the data. Like any other voluntary exercise in the corporate world this type of program falls apart at some point, does not achieve expectations, and/or is never able to scale across the business as it needs to.

Data governance provides the administrative infrastructure, oversight, and political wherewithal to implement the very important discipline of data stewardship.

As an executive you should consider asking the following questions of your business and IT leadership.

1) Do we have a data stewardship program today? If so, what does it entail? If not, why not?
2) Which positions within the organization currently participate in data stewardship activities? Which ones don't but need to?
3) How is the data stewardship program administered and managed?
4) Which processes and technologies do we use today to help orchestrate the data stewardship programs?
5) In your opinion what do we need to do to strengthen our data stewardship program?

Reporting

Every organization has different processes and technologies in place for creating, generating, and maintaining reports on business operations. Regardless of the tools and practices organizations use today there is normally room for improvement, sometimes vast improvement. After all, how many times does a division report from sales, marketing, and services accurately roll up to what the CxO is looking at?

For many organizations, the report creation and generation process can be a painful and costly venture. Aside from the material resources needed to create and maintain reports many businesses have found that over time they have amassed hundreds and thousands of reports, many that they no longer need, some that are duplicated, others that are inaccurate, and several that do not contain metadata. The problem is magnified when one bad report is built off another and when the intellectual properties that requested and created the reports are inconsistent, no longer with the company or have assumed other roles in the business.

Reporting environments of this nature are extremely costly to maintain and lead to a number of gaffes in reporting accuracy, duplication, and rework. The cost and problem becomes even more evident whenever organizations decide to move their reporting environment to a new system or application and the reports must be recreated. A good illustration of this is the example noted in the metadata section of this chapter.

Another good example of real life reporting problems comes from the visibility I had into a company for whom I consulted. Due to the company's reporting environment, the organization had under depreciated close to $10 million dollars in assets due to a report that had been built off the backs of other erroneous reports. The data itself was fairly accurate, but the baseline reports were constructed from inaccurate and inconsistent business rules and methods. The cost to identify and fix the problem was in the hundreds of thousands of dollars.

Data governance can play a significant role in the reporting process for organizations. Perhaps most import is the role it can play in overseeing these operations to ensure consistent business rules are applied, report requests are properly vetted between the business and IT, metadata is captured, customer definitions are consistent, and intellectual property is better centralized. In fact, reporting operations are one of those areas that organizations should seriously consider embracing within the framework of a data governance center of excellence.

As an executive you should consider asking the following questions of your business and IT leadership.

1) What are the major operational and economic challenges we are experiencing with reports today as it pertains to both routine and one-off reports?

2) What does our reporting process look like beginning with the original request through creation, generation, and maintenance of the report?

3) How are reports vetted between the business and IT today? How should they be?

4) How consistently are business rules applied between reports and to what level do we maintain metadata for each?

5) How many reports do we maintain today? How many are actively utilized by the business? Have we ever conducted and inventory of our reports? Should we?

Monitor, Measure, and Report

Like anything else in the business world, performance measurement is crucial. If an entity can quantify and effectively articulate the reason for their existence, and performance reflects progress, then odds are that upper management will take note and support the initiative. Data management activities are no exception and for good reason. By observing and quantifying data and business processes, it allows the business to better understand their data governance progress as well take actions to remediate data centric problems as they occur.

In the data management universe monitoring, measuring, and reporting pertains to the data itself. These functions typically involve developing benchmarks and gauging them against data quality results over time. After all, the quality of the data is perhaps the most tangible way to reflect the state of the data management ecosystem. This is generally accomplished through an automated set of profiling, data quality, reporting, and trending tools utilized by SMEs and data analysts. These practices make it possible for organizations to understand and respond to the condition of their data at any point in time.

These data management functions are also fundamental to capturing the metrics required to associate improvements in data outcomes to business performance. We will cover this topic in more detail in Chapter 10 when we discuss performance measurements. Until then it is important to note that data metrics are merely empty statistics unless an organization can correlate the statistics to business outcomes.

Data governance plays a key role in coordinating and overseeing the way organizations monitor, measure, and report on data outcomes and then interpret the results in terms the business can appreciate. In turn, this brings visibility into data operations and business results that likely do not exist today and are mission critical for any data asset management program.

As an executive you should consider asking the following questions of your business and IT leadership.

1) How do we monitor, measure, and report on our data today?
2) Do we leverage common technologies and business processes in capturing data metrics?
3) Do we connect data metrics back to business performance? If not, why not? If so, how do we do this?

4) What do we need to do to improve the way we monitor, measure, and report on data?

Chapter Summary

As you may have noticed, data management functions are highly interrelated and each have at least one common denominator; they all require a common governing body to enable them to be successful. With success comes efficiencies that breed cost reductions, cost avoidance, risk mitigation, and improved business performance.

Managing the workflow of the people, process, data, and technologies within and across the various data management domains is a tall task where most organizations fall short. While data governance does not solve all of these challenges out of the box, it does serve as the framework for which to begin to address the work flow within and between each of these data management functions. In turn, it clearly optimizes data and informational outcomes and overall business performance.

Chapter 6

Project Value

It is no secret that individual businesses spend millions of dollars annually on software license, maintenance, integration, education, training, and implementation for data centric solutions. Most of these expenditures are associated with projects that focus on MDM, ERP, CRM, CDI, BI, DW, EDW, data marts, data migration, and data integration. Equally recognized in the industry is that many of these same projects fall short of expectations, if not fail entirely, because organizations choose not to incorporate a data strategy and governance provisions into the project to ensure the best possible data outcomes.

Take for example the research conducted by various analytical groups over the past several years. This includes a report published by Forrester Research in 2008 titled, *Answers to Five Frequently Asked Questions about CRM Projects*,[3] the analyst group concluded that 28 percent of large enterprise CRM projects met or exceeded business expectations with the mid-market fairing a little better at 47 percent. Though times and surveys differ, the numbers are not all that different from 2001 when Gartner, Inc. first reported that over 50 percent of CRM projects fail to meet customer expectations.

Data warehouse failures also are well documented. In February of 2005, Gartner, Inc. announced that *"through 2007, more than 50 percent of data warehouse projects will have limited acceptance, or will be outright failures, as a result of a lack of attention to data quality issues."*[4] Keep in mind that data warehouses are the foundation to many business intelligence solutions. If you cannot get it right at the warehouse layer then poor outcomes for business intelligence are certain to follow suit.

---

[3] Gartner Inc., *Gartner Says More Than 50 Percent of Data Warehouse Projects Will Have Limited Acceptance or Will Be Failures Through 2007*, Press Release, Stamford, Connecticut, February 24, 2005 (http://www.gartner.com/it/page.jsp?id=492112)

[4] Forrester Research, *Answers to Five Frequently Asked Questions about CRM Projects*, William Band with Sharyn Leaver and Andrew Magarie, August 29, 2008. (http://www.forrester.com/rb/Research/answers_to_five_frequentl y_asked_questions_about/q/id/46432/t/2)

Determining success and failure can be very subjective and will vary from one organization and survey to the next. However, if you look at the numbers published throughout the industry they consistently push the 50 percent mark when it comes to organizations that do not achieve expectations or fail entirely with their data intensive projects. While there are many reasons for these disappointing outcomes, a common theme points to inadequate data quality, business participation, business requirements, and other activities tied to data governance as it relates to coordinating information quality across people, processes, technology, and lines of business.

Assume for a moment that the ROI for these projects are directly proportionate to the level of success they achieve. Does this mean that these same companies only achieve about 50 percent of their ROI goals? Now assume that these same projects had a well-defined data governance program incorporated into them and were able to improve project success rates by 15-30 percent, which is very reasonable. What does that do for project ROI? Does ROI go up 15-30 percent, or is it a matter of recovering this portion of the ROI that you already planned on? In any case, it is reasonable to assume that a solid data governance program can directly influence 15-30 percent of the ROI for data intensive projects.

Also keep in mind that while data governance requires an initial investment, the costs incurred can be spread across multiple projects as long as the discipline is treated as an overarching program within the organization. As a result, the ROI for each successive project should come quicker and at a lower overall cost to the organization.

I'll let you do the math but in the end it is reasonable to think that data governance can and will influence the success and ultimately the ROI for data intensive projects by 15-30 percent. Skeptical? - put your own number to the test. Either way, injecting data governance into the equation is sure to lead to substantial improvements in data and informational outcomes and ROI for these sorts of projects.

Data governance is important for all projects that involve information assets, but none more so than those that involve Master Data Management or creating a unified view of the business. These types of projects require a significant amount of decision making related to data standards, data ownership, data unification, survivorship, common data models, system of record, and much more. The role data governance plays in these environments cannot be underscored enough and will influence ROI substantially.

Chapter Summary

Yes, this is a short chapter. Primarily because there is no sense rehashing what you already know. In other words, project failures are well documented in the industry and you know better than anybody what you have spent on similar ventures within your own organization. What you may not realize is that data governance programs can and do have a material positive effect on your overall success and ROI for these very same projects. As such, organizations should be factoring data governance into their budget and plans for every data centric venture.

Chapter 7

Business Operations Value

Is This a Data Governance or Data Quality Value Proposition?

The value data governance brings to business operations is almost indistinguishable to the value data quality delivers to the same functions. In fact, some would argue that these are one-in-the-same since they deliver nearly identical benefits to various business activities. While both appear to convey the same value proposition, they do it on a different plane.

Data quality is most often defined and practiced within the parameters of a single project. These solitary implementations have an individual business purpose and normally involve a lone business function, technology application, and data domain. While technology alone will enable organizations to automate processes and make material strides in achieving quality outcomes, these tools have a ceiling as to what they can do for the business. Where data quality programs fall short is in their ability to manage the full data life cycle and operate on an enterprise level. This impedes their ability to incorporate influential business processes, enterprise data standards, establish policy, and engage cross-functional business interests that are imperative to optimizing data quality and business outcomes.

Data governance on the other hand is the catalyst for advancing data quality initiatives. Namely, it improves quality outcomes by enabling programs to break through politically charged cultures to address upstream and downstream people, processes, and technologies necessary to achieve optimal quality results. In addition, it brings visibility and insight to the company in a way that allows data quality initiatives to expand their footprint and influence to a number of traditional and not so traditional business functions across the organization. While conventional data quality is necessary in its own right, data governance enables it to grow and improve across the board.

The most powerful illustration of how data quality and data governance work together for common benefit goes to the heart of what is presented here. The goal for most organizations as reflected in these subsequent examples is to link related information across systems and lines of business to serve a specific business purpose. When this occurs, the value to the business can be substantial.

To be successful, data quality programs must cleanse, standardize, correct, and monitor data hygiene across multiple systems and data sources. In turn this function optimizes an organization's ability to establish and maintain data relationships within and across disparate systems. The reason is simple; data in one system is much easier to match in another system if they share common formats, codes, standards, rules, structure, and content. Data governance provides the layer of strategy and oversight required to create and manage policy, align business process, business units, and data owners so that data quality practices are applied consistently across all systems therefore making complex data relationships a reality.

Working together quality and governance improve business performance in a variety of ways. Due to their unique interdependency, the value proposition for business operations presented in this chapter reflects the value of both disciplines. Data quality represents the tactical and technically focused spot solution. Data governance characterizes the strategy, management, policy definition, and glue needed to optimize performance and grow data quality initiatives organization wide.

Sales & Marketing

Nearly every organization in the world has a sales and marketing arm to their business. Because of this, it should come as no surprise that these lines of business may be the biggest drivers for data governance outside of risk and compliance. Companies know that having the right information, at the right time, and for the right reason can drive material improvements in short and long term revenue streams. For sales and marketing this means having accurate and timely data along with an ability to understand and create reliable and even complex relationships between data elements, records, data sources, and other information in both the business to business (B2B) and business to consumer (B2C) environments.

While every organization and industry is different, the following represents the most common ways information assets drive the sales and marketing business. Furthermore, how improving data integrity leads to revenue generation and cost reductions in this space.

Improve Conversion Rates for Marketing Campaigns

Better information leads to improvements in market segmentation, house-holding, corporate house-holding and other methods used by marketing to focus campaigns on intended audiences. In turn, it raises revenues by increasing hit rates and the sales that flow from them. It also reduces the overall cost of the campaign by minimizing needless marketing to unintended parties.

One of the biggest obstacles for marketing teams to overcome is dealing with duplicate and inconsistent data. These data anomalies are created upstream by various people, processes, lines of business, and partners that interact with or supply the information. Marketing departments have a pretty good idea on how much additional revenue can be created if they are able to increase hit rates such that there is a measurable relationship between improving information quality, reducing data duplication, and an estimated or realized uptick in revenues.

A few years ago, I did work for a sales division of an automobile manufacturer and distributor that had an extensive data quality and governance issue. The net of the problem was that the company had a substantial amount of bad information in their database that was negatively impacting their sales, marketing, and customer service success. Upon review with the marketing and sales teams we discovered:

- At minimum, the company sent 80,000 new car marketing mailers to customers and prospects each quarter plus a few special promotions throughout the year.

- The rate on return mail was well over 10 percent.

- Though the company did not share the actual cost, the outlay to print and mail glossy, high quality automotive promotional materials was not cheap.

- The mail that reached its destination often missed its intended target for a number of reasons. For example, the promotion may have gone to the person or group that held title to the vehicle rather than to whom it was registered.

- When asked, marketing noted that for each 1 percent increase in their hit rates they would convert 16 new car sales per quarter or 64 annually. They knew this to be a fact based on their history and business model.

- The marketing, IT, and sales teams collectively felt that they could improve conversion rates by 1-4 percent if they implemented a data quality and governance program.

- The finance department validated that 64 new car sales per year would result in approximately $1,900,000 annually and if the team reached the high end of their goal at 4 percent improvement in hit rates it would result in additional sales revenues of $7.6 million per year.

The important thing to observe with this automotive example is that the business can help quantify the ROI when they are involved in the process. The data governance process brought these groups together fully exposing the opportunity and quantification of the business problem and solution.

Another case in point concerns a retail company that wanted to increase sales by improving their customer loyalty membership which meant they needed to improve their ability to market to this group. The company was faced with several quality issues including an 18 percent duplication rate of customer records. The company was further concerned about their limited ability to fix and control upstream processes that were contributing to the problem.

To resolve the issue the organization instituted both data governance and data quality programs. Within the first twelve months, the company reduced duplication rates down to 4 percent and observed their loyalty membership enrollment climb by 6 percent. Best of all, this initiative is credited with improving marketing campaigns and generating new sales revenues of $750,000 dollars by the end of the first year. While the financial impact is compelling, I found it equally interesting that this company went to great lengths to measure their business success from these programs which is certainly not the norm in today's world. At the same time, the company was not willing to go public with the information because of the competitive nature of their business.

Telemarketing & Telesales

Like any marketing campaign, the better the information the better the conversion rates for selling products and services. With telemarketing and telesales the benefits of good information can lead to an increase in revenue generation, a downturn in operational costs, and an improved corporate image. Increased revenues come in the form of selling more products and services. Cost reduction is normally associated with decreasing the number of calls and resources needed to achieve revenue goals. In addition, good information can minimize negative public perception by reducing the number of calls to unintended and uninterested parties.

Take for instance the automotive example explained earlier. In addition to the 80,000 marketing mailers sent out on a quarterly basis, the telesales team sent out 15,000 mailers each month to selected customers. The telesales group would follow up the monthly mailing by calling each of the 15,000 customers that received the promotional literature. The purpose of the calls was to upsell extended service agreements, routine maintenance, additional options, accessories, products, and services. Because telesales was working from some of the same bad data as the rest of the sales and marketing organization they encountered several problems.

- Calls were going to people about the type of vehicle they owned when in fact they purchased an entirely different type or class of automobile.

- Calls were being placed regarding overdue maintenance even though the customer had already completed the maintenance at the company's facilities.

- Individuals were receiving calls about purchasing additional options before they even took delivery on the new vehicle at which time the options would be explained to them again.

- Calls were being placed to individuals that were deceased.

- Customers were receiving multiple calls because call history was inconsistently recorded.

- Many calls could not be completed because of incorrect or missing phone numbers.

- Calls were going to lienholders instead of individuals that held the vehicle registration.

- Some customers were receiving calls on vehicles they no longer owned and of which had been traded in at the company facilities when the customer purchased a new car from them.

- Return mail was estimated at a little less than 10 percent.

The problems encountered by telesales go beyond customer name and address and point to the heart of product, maintenance records, telephone numbers, call history, purchase and trade-in history, and latency of information. In talking with the telesales team, they were clearly exasperated with the high percentage of incorrect numbers, talking to the wrong people, and trying to sell the wrong mix of products and services to the individuals. It was further acknowledged that this environment was a significant contributor to employee turnover among the telesales team.

Unfortunately, this portion of the project was never quantified in financial terms though the affect on the business is self-evident. In this scenario bad data impeded the ability of telesales to upsell additional products and services. Management clearly acknowledged the negative impact it was having on the business as a whole given that maintenance and service revenues are a large part of the automobile industry. In addition, the costs incurred for recruiting, hiring, and training telesales agents were recognized by management to be excessive.

While the impact to the business, operations, and customer satisfaction is obvious, the important thing to note is that telemarketing/telesales operations must have access to quality and timely data. In this case, it was a need to access consumer, purchasing, maintenance, trade-in, and product data. Once again, it takes data quality initiatives to get the information right and it takes a data governance discipline to oversee the people, process, technologies, and business alignment necessary to bring it all together.

Reduce Cost, Cycle Time, and Churn of Marketing Campaigns

The time and cost required to produce a marketing campaign can be extensive and much of this is attributed directly to the data. I have been privy to many situations where marketing analysts spent weeks, even months, preparing data for a single campaign. A lot of this time is spent fixing the information, de-duplicating records, performing segmentation, and augmenting the data with demographics or other information from third party sources.

For some companies, this is a ritual that happens on a monthly or quarterly basis. Often times with the same bad, outdated data. This also is a great exercise for the IT team to experience. I have seen many eye opening, jaw-dropping epiphanies take place when IT folks sit down with marketing analysts and actually see firsthand how data is prepared and used in campaigns. The only thing better than witnessing this is seeing the troubleshooting and progress that comes from such an exercise.

A good data governance program brings IT and the business together and can improve upstream data quality in a way that reduces the cycle time and costs associated with preparing data for marketing campaigns as well as help generate better results for the campaign itself.

Sales and Marketing within a Reseller Business Model

It is almost assured that whenever a business model incorporates non-captive agents and/or high volume third party resellers, especially at point-of-sale (POS), that certain processes, practices, and data challenges are going to transpire within sales and marketing. These activities are not always healthy and include some of the following practices that lead to immediate short term gain but produce long range problems within a business.

- Providers of the product/service often have minimum/insufficient requirements for resellers to collect customer and product information. The mentality is "just get the order completed, we can't slow down the sales process."

- Resellers will often capture and transmit incomplete, inconsistent, and missing data (just enough to process the sales transaction).

- Much of the data collected to process a sale becomes useless to marketing, sales, customer service, and support operations when it is incomplete, inaccurate, duplicated, or missing.

- Extensive manual intervention is required for both partners and the company to reconcile sales numbers and sales commissions due to the volume and inconsistent data between the organizations.

The primary business impact to a company working under these circumstances is that they substantially compromise their ability to market to and support customers. As a result, it restricts their capacity to upsell warranties, renewals, upgrades, accessories, complimentary products, services, and more.

Another set of problems that arise from this business model is the cost to reconcile sales and sales commissions within and between organizations. I have observed instances where companies employ multiple people that spend weeks reconciling information every month or quarter in order to give credit where credit is due. In many cases, both the company that provides the product or service and the reseller execute this process.

While the reconciliation process alone can be expensive the price of overpaying commissions can be even greater. A complex sales environment of this nature is also a breeding ground for fraudulent sales activities. Ask any organization that has a intricate sales model and there is inevitably a fraudulent event that has taken place at some point in time that the business is reluctant to talk about.

Let me be clear that I am not here to say a reseller model is a bad thing, after all, what company is going to run from a proven and dependable revenue stream? My point is that it is not what you do but how you do it. Given this state-of-affairs, companies have an opportunity to maintain their revenue stream yet increase after sales revenues, decrease the cost of doing business with resellers, and improve partner relations. This can be accomplished by implementing reasonable and achievable data quality controls within the sales process and the technologies used to facilitate these transactions. I say reasonable and achievable because data collection at the POS is a delicate balance between what information can realistically be collected, the format and standards that can be applied, and affect (if any) it can have on the initial transaction and customer experience.

To optimize overall revenue in these situations, an organization must first be willing to evaluate the entire sales process and weigh the overall benefits to the organization in a holistic, non-partisan way. For example, the process and procedures implemented for transacting third party business are normally dominated by the sales organization with little regard to how it impacts the rest of the organization's ability to generate future revenue or support the customer base they create. The issue does not rest solely on the sales department. Trust me, I have personally worked in the sales world for many years and I fully understand and appreciate the importance of closing the deal. While I value the "just get the order in the door" mentality by no means should this be the only argument or criteria for how a company conducts business. In fact, many times companies hide behind this sales ideology and end up short-changing the overall company business.

Data governance and data quality play an extremely important role in this environment. Data quality can improve the condition of the data at multiple points in the sales process. Data governance can help the organization gain visibility into the entire process, evaluate the comprehensive affect it has on the business, and develop and oversee data strategies and solutions that enhance the overall revenue generation of the company.

Customer Buying Preferences

Organizations are always searching for ways to enhance their understanding of a customer's personal preferences in order to better target their sales and marketing activities to the customer. For example, in the travel and hospitality industry the more an agent understands when, where, and how a customer likes to travel the better the agent can match travel promotions to the interests of their clientele. This can include customer preferences for destinations, time of year, hotel amenities, favorite events, and more.

Another example pertains to the gaming industry where organizations are continuously trying to identify personal preferences and habits of their patrons. This includes where one gambles, the time of day, the machines or gaming tables preferred, gift shops and stores frequented, choice of restaurants and cuisine, favorite entertainment and excursions, hotel room preferences, and much more.

I have had the privilege of working on data related projects within both of these industries and it is clear that the better information organizations have available about their customers the better they can drive repeat business and upsell a number of products and services. Companies in this space seldom go public with data centric programs but are known to spend hundreds of thousands of dollars and more annually to improve data outcomes.

One organization I worked with in the travel industry goes as far as to leverage their data governance program as a competitive differentiator when working with prospective partners. The story the business conveys is that of a company that is taking exceptional measures to manage their data and as a result provide better revenue generating opportunities for their partners.

Data quality and data governance are the key to delivering the right information at the right time and for the right reason in support of these business models. A strong data quality and governance program can easily add hundreds of thousands if not millions of dollars in additional revenue to the bottom line of companies in this space. This also applies to a number of other industries where moving from a reliance on general consumer data to more precise personal buying preferences is a crucial business driver.

Other Sales & Marketing Opportunities

The list of opportunities for driving revenues and reducing cost through data management in the world of sales and marketing seems endless. At the end of the day, most opportunities in this space focus on improving marketing campaigns, advertisement, promotional strategies, lead generation, and simply knowing your customer for a number of real good business reasons. While not necessarily widespread, the following represents other areas where organizations have found value in data quality and governance within sales and marketing.

- Identification of high value customers
- Improve research and product development
- Improve sales territory mapping
- Understand and apply common pricing models across domains
- Improve customer access to products and services
- Improve sales forecasting
- Identification and analysis of sale vs. no sale
- Competitive analysis

Risk and Compliance

Many of the drivers, especially the early business drivers for data governance come from the areas of risk and compliance. This is especially true with respect to the financial industry where risk is at the core of their very existence. These organizations are known to establish formal risk and compliance offices. These offices are essentially a derivative of data governance with a specific focus yet a common business purpose. Since the early adoption of this discipline, other industries have also recognized the merit of this practice and have found ways to leverage data governance and quality to minimize risk, detect fraud, and drive compliance.

Organizations can be subject to hundreds of regulations from government, industry, or their own corporate policies. To meet these various demands it is necessary to accurately capture and report information to the designated agencies and authorities. Failure to comply with these regulations can lead to costly penalties, fines, legal actions, audits, sanctions, lost jobs, and even jail time.

For most businesses the key to compliance is being able to collect, safeguard, assemble, and report the required information in an accurate, timely, and cost effect fashion. Unfortunately, compliance information is often scattered across the organization making the process of collecting the data, scrubbing it, putting it into a report, and retaining an audit trail along the way a very costly and complex venture.

Data quality and data governance are known to improve this process and the accuracy of the subsequent results. In turn, it reduces the risk to the organization. While there are literally thousands of examples of risk and regulations that dictate compliance the following represent some of the most common that affect organizations worldwide.

Data Privacy & Security

Nearly every organization handles personal and financial information of its members, customers, partners, and/or employees. This data is at routine risk of theft, loss, and fraud. Especially in today's world of laptops, flash drives, and hackers, it is all too easy for sensitive data to fall into the wrong hands.

I have done work for more than one business that has had over 15,000 spreadsheets and desktop databases and over 10,000 PDF's, JPEG files, and Word documents containing various forms of consumer data. Much of the information is circulated through the business via e-mail, shared servers, and nearly everyone in the company is working off a laptop. In every instance the entire environment lacked any meaningful oversight. Does this sound familiar? Whether or not this reflects your organization, you have to appreciate the nature of this challenge and the growing risk within your business.

Whatever the breech in security might be, it is sure to lead extensive direct and indirect costs to the organization. Direct costs come in the form of notification of the breach such as mailing letters of response, investigation of the incident, class action litigation, civil suits, replacing payment cards, lost productivity and even hiring staff to manage the problem, marketing campaigns to restore consumer confidence, and reimbursement of other miscellaneous costs. Indirect costs come with the negative publicity that appears over the Internet, on the nightly news, and in the local, national, and international newspapers. How do you put a value on this? It is not always straightforward but the following examples may help quantify the risk for your organization.

According to the *2010 U.S. Cost of a Data Breach Study*[5] conducted by the Ponemon Institute and sponsored by Symantec Research, the average cost of a data breach for a United States company was approximately $7.2 million dollars in 2010, up seven percent over 2009. The cost per compromised record increased to $214 dollars, up from $204 dollars in 2009. The most expensive data breach was $35.3 million dollars and the least expensive being $780,000 dollars.

The study goes on to say that best practices for avoiding a data breach include:

- Identifying and classifying confidential information
- Educate employees on information protection policies and procedures

---

[5] Ponemon Institute sponsored by Symantec Research, *2010 Annual Study: U.S. Cost of Data Breach*, March 8, 2011 (http://www.ponemon.org/blog/post/cost-of-a-data-breach-climbs-higher)

- Hold employees accountable for following policies and procedures
- Integrate information protection practices into business processes

Can you say data governance? The governance discipline clearly plays a leadership role in establishing and overseeing these and other best practices.

These findings can easily overlay the incidents that have made the news over the last few years with countless companies losing back-up tapes, having their system hacked, leaving laptops unattended, losing laptops, employees having unneeded access to sensitive data (WikiLeaks), and falling victim to employee theft. However, one particular example is that of Certegy.

In 2010 Certegy, a subsidiary of Fidelity National Information Services, agreed to a settlement with the Florida Attorney General's office to upgrade its data security technology and processes after a major security breach in 2007 exposed the personal, banking, and credit card information of 5.9 million customers. This was a case where an employee stole the data and sold it to outside marketing organizations. The settlement included $1 million dollars to the State of Florida not to mention the cost the company incurred to litigate and perform damage control around the incident. One requirement of the settlement was for the company to comply with Payment Card Industry (PCI) security standards.

The PCI is a global, vendor neutral council founded in 2006 for the purpose of establishing payment card security standards worldwide. While this group has no real power to regulate, many legislative agencies embrace their standards as in the case of the State of Florida. The PCI Data Security Standards clearly define what organizations need to do to safeguard information at both a technical and process level. While these standards relate to the payment card industry, many of their best practices transcend to the security of other sensitive data.

As the State of Florida and the PCI standards indicate, data security is as much about process as it is technology. A data governance program mitigates risk such as this by raising the level of awareness and visibility into the practices of an organization. It also validates and strengthens compliance to standards such as the PCI. Finally, it helps facilitate the implementation and monitoring of these practices within large, complex data and business environments.

Costly security breaches do not always come in the form of malicious attacks nor is it always about personal information. Take for instance the large healthcare organization that shared with me their reasons for starting a data governance program. The hospital system had finished up a large technology implementation about 18 months earlier that put all their hospitals and most of their affiliate organizations on the same patient-charge-capture system. About a year after the implementation, an individual in a subsidiary hospital mistakenly changed information that negatively impacted rates and reimbursements for the entire health system. By the time the institution discovered the problem they had lost more than $2 million dollars. Upon review the person should never had had system privileges that allowed him to change the information.

While data governance is not intended to replace an existing data security discipline in an organization it can certainly augment the practice by identifying potential hazards, defining access privileges, and weaving best practices into the corporate culture. In other situations, data governance may be the springboard for formalizing sub disciplines around managing personal information, PCI, and other aspects of data security.

Another way data governance provides value in this space is to drive awareness, answers, and actions around how third party providers and partners treat company data. As the Pomenon study indicates, over 40 percent of data breaches come from third parties. Data governance programs should consider extending their reach into the policies and practices of partners and partners-to-be in order to mitigate risk going forward.

Financial Risk & Regulation

The financial services industry bases its entire livelihood on lending money, investing capital, managing the risk of return, and dealing with regulatory compliance. Companies in this space have a long list of activities where they proactively assess risk, such as:

- Credit risk
- Market risk
- Solvency
- Liquidity risk
- Systemic risk
- Operational risk

The profitability of financial institutions is rooted in their competency to assess various forms of risk. Most of these businesses have a formal risk and compliance division within their organization to support these needs. It also is why many organizations are adding official data quality and data governance to their infrastructure. Companies know that accurate and timely credit information can mean the difference between compliance or noncompliance, and posting a profit or loss, sometimes in the millions of dollars.

There are far too many financial industry regulations to cover here but there are a few worth mentioning.

The Basel II and III Accords are a set of international banking law recommendations made by the Basel Committee on Banking Supervision. As these recommendations are progressively implemented across countries worldwide, they pose new challenges for financial establishments and regulators. Basel II and III focus on implementing standards for how much capital banks must keep readily available to safeguard their overall solvency. Because this is a very complex process, banks must implement new processes and technologies that can effectively collect, track, and report on information that satisfies these new requirements.

The Accords dictate mandatory levels of cash reserves that banks must have on hand to cover existing loans as well as to issue new lines of credit. This is intended to safeguard institutions in the event that a substantial portion of loans default. Data quality and data governance are critical in this regard as the accuracy and timeliness of information informs the entire process. This is especially true for organizations with business transactions conducted across national borders.

Other major regulations in recent years include:

- Fair and Accurate Credit Transaction Act (FACTA) – United States law signed in 2003 that allows consumers better access to credit reports and provides improved identity protection, fraud prevention and alerts, and restoration of credit history.

- Dodd-Frank Wall Street Reform and Consumer Protection Act (Dodd-Frank) – United States law signed in 2010 that focuses on streamlining the financial regulatory process, increasing systemic risk oversight, and driving transparency and accountability.

Data governance not only helps drive accurate results in support of these core business processes, it demonstrates a new layer of transparency and compliance that politicians, regulators, and the public have demanded of the financial industry in recent years.

Healthcare Privacy & Security

There are a number of healthcare privacy and security laws that have been enacted worldwide. The most visible may be the United States healthcare legislation covered in the Health Insurance Portability and Accounting Act (HIPAA). This law covers a number of things within the healthcare system to include protecting workers and families when they change or lose their jobs, invoking standards for national electronic healthcare transactions, reducing fraud, creating single identifiers for employers, providers, and insurance plans. As it pertains to this book, the most important HIPAA topic relates to its security and privacy requirements.

Every organization must safeguard and protect the medical privacy of its employees, members, customers, and patients. Releasing this information to the public or unauthorized persons can certainly lead to fines and costly civil litigation. This applies to both electronic and paper documents.

HIPAA is enforced by the Health and Human Services (HHS) department of the United States Government. In February of 2011 the Office of Civil Rights (OCR), a department within HHS, fined Massachusetts General Hospital $1 million dollars for losing the records of 192 patients. They also fined Cignet Health of Maryland a record $4.3 million dollars for refusing 41 patients from gaining access to their medical records. While $3 million of Cignet's fine was attributed to their unwillingness to cooperate with OCR, the other $1.3 million was assessed due to not providing patient records within 30 days and no later than 60 days of when the records were requested by the patient as prescribed by law.

While these examples pertain to healthcare organizations they clearly apply to any company, agency, or practice that handles personal healthcare information. Furthermore, it can apply to most countries around the world that have enacted their own privacy and security laws. For the United States, the message on the street is that HHS is getting serious about enforcing HIPAA laws and their recent actions certainly point to stronger enforcement going forward.

A data governance program helps organizations manage risk around sensitive healthcare information to ensure it is safeguarded and that the information is released in compliance with HIPAA and other laws.

Fraud

Unfortunately, data and fraud go together all too often. There are literally thousands of ways to commit fraud through the manipulation of data and information. While fraud statistics are historically hard to quantify, average cost estimates for many industries range from 3-10 percent of gross revenues and can fluctuate with economic conditions.

For many businesses, fraud is a non-event, even an unthinkable one until it happens. For this reason, tangibly measuring and predicting the direct impact data quality and governance has on reducing fraudulent activities is an unrealistic expectation for most businesses. Consider if you hired a security guard to watch the front entrance of your business. How can you quantify whether the position deterred crime? If the presence of a security guard does deter crime, it is still difficult (impossible) to project the financial savings this service provides. However, this does not mean it was not a good decision to hire the security guard. The same holds true with data quality and governance. It is reasonable to think that improving data content and the transparency around data management and business processes will have a material affect on mitigating risk within an organization. Just ask the analysts and others in your organization tasked with monitoring, preventing, predicting, and uncovering fraudulent activities to protect the company.

A good example of fraud and governance comes from two large retailers I was once involved with. Both companies have a large number of stores, warehouses, and distribution facilities across North America and both spend millions of dollars annually on claims related to property, casualty, theft, liability, and more. In each case these corporations know that a good percentage of claims are fraudulent and/or preventable and are struggling to aggregate the information they need in order to accurately assess future risk and fully understand the opportunities for reducing it. Fraud alone was estimated in the tens of millions of dollars for both organizations. Because of the way information is collected and spread across multiple parties and systems, it requires a concentrated effort around data quality and governance to resolve this challenge.

Data quality and data governance play an instrumental role in preventing and uncovering fraudulent activities. Data quality improves informational content that allows analysts and systems to better detect data anomalies and link questionable relationships between individuals, entities, transactions, and events. By its very nature data governance is a fraud deterrent due to the way it creates a culture of transparency and visibility into data, processes, and lines of business that would normally be off limits in a traditional organization structure.

Terrorism & Sanctions

Many countries have laws that prohibit its residents and companies from doing business with designated foreign organizations and individuals. Perhaps sanctions have been placed on an organization or an individual has been classified as a suspected terrorist. In the United States, the Office of Foreign Assets Control (OFAC) administers this process. One of the functions of the OFAC is to issue a Specially Designated Nationals List (SDN or OFAC List) of organizations and individuals that United States residents are prohibited from engaging in business.

Many companies use the SDN to match against their client, prospect, passenger, vendor, and member databases to identify SDN's. The airlines and the Transportation Security Administration (TSA) run passenger lists against the SDN and other lists to detect possible terrorists. Data standardization, record duplication controls, and sophisticated matching algorithms are instrumental to identifying a name on the SDN to a possible but not always straightforward match or set of matches in a company database. Because of this, organizations that compare their customers or business partners against the SDN must have sound quality and governance practices established around their own data first before they even compare their list against the SDN.

OFAC fines and penalties can be substantial and for the financial industry can equal and exceed the amount of the illegal transaction. The potential impact to a community and the lives of individuals is immeasurable.

Occupational Safety and Health Administration (OSHA)

OSHA is charged with enforcing safety and health regulation in the United States. While there are some exemptions, many companies are required to keep records and report on things such as workplace injuries, chemical exposure, accidents, and deaths. In industries such as manufacturing, large retail and healthcare this can be a challenging process. If organizations fail to maintain accurate records or comply with reporting standards, they can be subject to OSHA penalties and fines. Even if fines are not imposed, the cost of an OSHA audit and appeals process can be costly to an organization that has not managed their data and information in this area. Data governance and quality can play a role in this process, especially for the large organizations with complex OSHA requirements and/or consistent challenges in this arena.

Sarbanes-Oxley Act (Sarbanes/SOX)

The Sarbanes-Oxley Act of 2002 imposes regulation over public companies and accounting firms in order to reduce the risk of scandal and corruption like that which plagued the corporate world in the late 1990's and early 2000's. The primary purpose of this act was to restore public confidence in the securities market.

In what many saw as a revolutionary step, Congress included criminal penalties for individuals that are found guilty of performing wrongdoing. This is reflected in section 802 of the legislation.

"Whoever knowingly alters, destroys, mutilates, conceals, covers up, falsifies, or makes a false entry in any record, document, or tangible object with the intent to impede, obstruct, or influence the investigation or proper administration of any matter within the jurisdiction of any department or agency of the United States or any case filed under title 11, or in relation to or contemplation of any such matter or case, shall be fined under this title, imprisoned not more than 20 years, or both."

There is also a provision in the act for protecting whistleblowers. The point is that this law intends to drive transparency, accuracy, and accountability at all levels and for all people. The very nature of data quality (accuracy) and data governance (transparency and accountability) promotes a healthy environment that compliments Sarbanes. In some cases it may even keep people out of jail!

There are countless ways for data quality and governance to support risk and compliance initiatives. Incorporating these disciplines reduces an organization's overall risk, improves compliance, and the decreases the associated costs of doing business.

Customer Service

Customer service is at core of the business model for many organizations. As such, mastering this core competency is often the difference between leading or lagging behind the competition. This is especially critical for customer facing businesses and those that operate high volume call centers such as retail, telecommunications, and the airlines. In some cases, service may even be tracked by analysts, watchdog groups, or other public forums where an incremental bump up or down can have a significant effect on the business.

Some may argue this point but at the end of the day most customer service organizations want to accomplish one (or all) of the following: drive customer retention and renewals; minimize returns and cancellations; upsell products and services; and keep costs down. In support of these goals, service organizations often measure a number of things that gage their performance.

- Customer retention
- Sales per call
- Revenue per call
- Returns and cancellations
- Cost per call
- Number of calls
- Duration of calls
- Transfer rates
- Response time
- On hold time
- Abandonment rate
- Number of escalated calls
- Lost opportunities
- Error and rework percentage
- Self service percentage
- Employee retention

To the credit of the customer service field this profession has developed some strong measures of their activities and that of their customers. Because of this, one can go to a customer service manager and quickly comprehend how this business measures performance and how data and information influence business outcomes.

A formula commonly applied to customer service operations implies a relationship between data quality and governance activities and the metrics listed above. As governance initiatives are rolled out or improved, the metrics will also improve; say by 2-10 percent. In turn, customer satisfaction will increase, sales will increase, the cost to staff operations may go down because fewer people are needed and more people will stay longer which reduces hiring and training costs.

I once worked with a company that had but a single business driver and that was to improve customer retention. The organization had done their homework and by their estimations every one percent swing in customer retention meant either a $5 million dollar annual revenue increase or decrease. It was imperative for the company to make sure the data made available to their customer support operations and call centers was accurate and timely. While the organization never officially published the results of their quality and governance program, the word within their call center operations was that their program was credited with improving customer retention by approximately .75 percent in the first full year or approximately $3.75 million dollars in additional annual revenues.

Data quality and governance are known to improve customer services operations in ways that lower operational costs, drive revenue, retain customers, and improve goodwill through public perception.

Order-to-Cash

Every organization, especially in the private sector, has an order-to-cash (OTC) process of some nature and it normally follows the path of:

- Sales order (create and book)
- Fulfillment (pick order – physical and electronic)
- Ship order (distribution)
- Invoice (billing)
- Payment
- Collection
- Sales commissions paid (internal and third party partners)

That said, there are a number of ways that companies implement this basic model. For example, a cash POS transaction at your local grocery store will look different than how an insurance company processes the creation, underwriting, and payment of a new policy or how a manufacturing facility collects and fulfills on orders. However, at the end of the day all are fulfilling a sales order, collecting payment for it, possibly producing or reordering goods, and in some cases paying commissions on the sale.

The challenge with this process is that it spans multiple people, departments, and systems related to sales, materials management, purchasing, accounts payable, accounts receivable, legal, and others depending on the type of business. It is further complicated when sales orders come from third party partners where information and data formats are often inconsistent with the parent business.

There are a number of problems that stem from this model that include incorrect product shipments, wrong shipping location, inaccurate invoices, incorrect payment, untimely payments, or incorrect sales commissions. Collectively, the time, cost, and rework associated with this process from start to finish can be extensive and has a negative business impact in three primary ways.

1) Ties up company cash
2) Adds unnecessary overhead
3) Erodes customer and partner satisfaction

In a March 2008 study by the Aberdeen Group entitled *"The Order-to-Cash Cycle, Integrating Business Process to Improve Operational Performance,"* [6] this research and analyst organization reports that 56 percent of companies surveyed are driven to improve the OTC process in order to improve cash flow. It also goes on to say that leading, best-of-class companies (top 20 percent of aggregate performance scores) have better control over their cash and invoicing for their products and services.
The study indicates that leading companies have common performance metrics in five key areas.

(1) Process (standardized enterprise-wide procedures)

---

[6] Aberdeen Group, A Harte-Hanks Company, *The Order-to-Cash Cycle, Integrating Business Process to Improve Operational Performance,* March 31, 2008 (http://www.aberdeen.com/Aberdeen-Library/4671/RA-order-to-cash.aspx)

(2) Organization (cross department collaboration)

(3) Knowledge management (visibility to order, delivery, and billing information)

(4) Technology (the selection of appropriate tools and effective deployment of those tools to streamline and integrate processes and minimize manual intervention)

(5) Performance management (the ability of the organization to measure results to improve business)

Do these areas sound a little like data governance? The similarities are striking and that is why data governance and quality play a key role in the order-to-cash process. Both can facilitate the standardization and management of data standards and processes to drive the desired business outcomes.

Taxes, Fees, and Payments

Data governance has attracted the public sector through the need to accurately collect taxes and fees and pay benefits and refunds. While this sounds straightforward, the reality is that public agencies have to accomplish these tasks within a complex maze of local, regional, and national agencies; all with their own jurisdictions, systems, politics, agendas, and rules of law.

For some agencies, un-recovered revenue is estimated to be in the millions to tens of millions of dollars annually. Agencies that fall into this category already know the root of the problem; it is because their systems and sister agencies do not integrate and communicate with each other. The consequence is that public agencies do not have a single view of the citizen or taxpayer and therefore cannot effectively identify underpayment, overpayment, fraud, or abuse of taxes, fees, and benefits.

For example, I am familiar with a state revenue agency that established a data governance initiative to bring together accurate and timely information from several internal and external agencies. The primary purpose behind this initiative was to capture lost property tax revenues. Within the first year of the program, the agency recovered more than $4 million dollars in tax revenues that were misreported by taxpayers. Under a business-as-usual model the agency could not access or identify the relationships between data and the taxpayer. It took a governance program to open up the opportunity for collecting the missed taxes.

The financial impact on the state revenue agency also extended to cash flow. The organization fully acknowledged that they did not have a holistic view of taxpaying entities. As a result, refunds were often sent to citizens and businesses that also had an offsetting liability to the state. The governance program helped reduce these incidences and improve the cash flow for the agency.

Improper payments may be the biggest overall challenge for the public sector. This includes payments to the wrong recipient, incorrect payment amount, abuse of funds, and payments made without supporting documentation. The United States government reported that in fiscal year 2010 it made $125 billion dollars in improper payments to individuals, businesses, and contractors.[7] This accounted for 5.49 percent of all payments made by the federal government. In addition, several million dollars of these payments went to dead people.

In response to the problem, the President of the United States recently signed into law the Improper Payments Elimination and Recovery Act (IPERA). IPERA sets guidelines for federal agencies to reduce improper payments and accelerate recovery of lost funds. Most of the guidelines focus on public communication, transparency, technology oversight, increased audits, and compliance reviews.

Nothing within IPERA addresses data governance or how agencies must work together to integrate and share information or how data policy will be enforced. The federal plan looks good on paper and sounds good in the press but lacks the glue (data governance) to make it work. Agencies will continue to operate in silo conditions where system, data, and intellectual property remain fragmented. Furthermore, much of the solution will come in the form of increased audits and reviews, which are labor intensive and reactive rather than proactive measures.

Like any data centric project, it is sure to fall short of expectations or fail entirely if an overarching data governance program is not established. Such a program must be inclusive of a strong

---

[7] United States Government, Payment Accuracy, Official Website of the United States Government, 2011 (http://paymentaccuracy.gov/)

oversight branch (Office of Information Asset Management?) to enforce interagency cooperation and data policy compliance.

My question to other agencies is what percentage of your annual payments is considered improper and what might the cost be to the agency? Chances are that data governance will have a positive, short and long-term affect on reducing improper payments and improving collections and cash flow from taxes and fees.

Mail & Transport

It could be said that the first attempts to implement data quality came from the mail and transportation industry where tangible returns have long been associated with getting a mailing address right. This practice still holds true today. Having a correct address enables companies to decrease costs by gaining access to postal discounts, reducing duplicate mailings, minimizing errant mail, and cutting back the cost of handling return mail. This is especially true for large mailing operations associated with in-house marketing campaigns, mass customer correspondence, mail houses, and large scale shipping activities. From a business perspective getting the address right not only equates to cost reduction but also increases revenues when it comes to improving marketing campaign hit rates and conversions.

Postage discounts in the United States can be noteworthy enough that organizations will invest hundreds of thousands of dollars or more in technology and business process in order to qualify for them. Discounts worldwide vary by postal authority and are normally based on a number of factors such as volume, destination, type of mail or package, address certification, whether mail is pre-sorted, has a printed barcode, company has non-profit status, and/or complies with mover update requirements, and other factors.

I once consulted with a large insurance company that presents a classic example of how data quality and data governance converge to drive down mailing costs. This institution had twelve clearly defined data sources that held customer information, including addresses in each. Address standardization technologies and procedures were only being applied to one data source while the other eleven were floundering in address chaos.

As part of the consulting process, I asked to meet with the business along with the IT folks in charge of their new data quality project. A dozen IT people attended the meeting and only one business representative. The business person had only ever met one, possibly two, of the IT people prior to the meeting. After reviewing the data flow and challenges associated with the twelve customer data sources the business person in attendance shared with the group that the company had 9 people employed full time to deal with return mail! The experience was eye opening if not shocking for everyone in attendance. The business person gained visibility into the source of the return mail problems and the IT folks came away with an appreciation for the business impact. It was clear that IT and the business players were disjointed but once they were brought together they were able to identify and quantify the magnitude of the problem on the spot.

While I was not engaged with this company long enough to find out what their eventual savings amounted to, they did acknowledge that they had an opportunity to reduce headcount by 3-6 people. Based on the circumstances it was realistic to assume that the company could save nearly $1 million dollars annually, over and above staff reductions, in postage and other operational efficiencies.

This example not only demonstrates the value that data quality brings to the mail and transport industry but also how the data governance process drove visibility and exposed the problem by bringing the right people in the business and IT together. It also reinforces how data quality is often implemented within a single project or data source without consideration for how the same or similar data is collected or leveraged across other parts of the business.

Supply Chain

The supply chain refers to the movement of product and services between suppliers and involves activities such as production, purchasing, distribution, inventory control, distribution, logistics, and more. In today's world, companies are beginning to employ data quality and data governance in the supply chain to reduce costs.

Two of the best examples of lowering costs in this space reside in purchasing, especially large, decentralized purchasing operations. From a quality perspective, the first opportunity comes with linking common vendor information so that the purchasing organization can better recognize a vendor's corporate hierarchy and distribution channels. This situates the purchasing arm of the organization to improve its capacity to roll up and summarize their acquisition history with vendors, subsidiaries, and partners. In turn, organizations can leverage the information to negotiate more favorable pricing and terms with its suppliers.

Another common application for quality is to cleanse and normalize product information so that purchasing departments can gain visibility into where they might be able to standardize on similar products. From there organizations can negotiate better pricing and even consolidate the number of vendors they utilize. These benefits also extend to inventory control where costs go down as the number of products on the shelf decrease.

I once worked with an organization that was building and maintaining aircraft for several branches of a parent organization. Their data challenge had to do with airplane parts. The parts were purchased by various divisions within the parent organization using separate computer systems and stocked in a number of warehouses around the world. Each division used their own set of product codes. Some products had multiple manufacturers and their codes were not recorded in a consistent format, or they were missing entirely. Consequently, the company experienced a number of problems from being out of stock, overstocked, ordering incorrect products, using multiple vendors for the same parts, to manufacturing and maintenance delays.

To fix the problem the organization building and maintaining the aircraft had to develop a data governance program involving each division of the parent company. From there they instituted a corporate data quality program that focused on product taxonomy, standards, clean up, and business process improvement.

Now, if your purchasing department is like those of most organizations they will be quick to declare that they have things under control and there is no need to get involved with their data. Fortunately or unfortunately, history says otherwise and is supported by examples where anomalies within vendor and product databases abound. This is where data governance steps in, working to create business alignment and visibility into data sources that are normally off limits, such as purchasing information.

The supply chain can be an intricate process and there are a variety of ways that data governance can drive down costs within this environment.

Social and Human Services

The public sector has unique information requirements for managing, delivering, and reporting on social programs and human services. Many of these data and information outcomes are measured in terms of how it affects people's lives rather than in financial metrics.

One example is data governance's ability to lower crime rates and improve emergency response times. Many law enforcement agencies and emergency medical services (EMS) are implementing governance programs that focus on bringing together information from a number of sources to predict where crime or emergencies are likely to occur. These agencies collect information from one another, such as demographics, data on weather, road conditions, local events, time of year, economic conditions, and more to position resources in areas where events are most likely to take place. In the case of crime, this allows police to target particular areas for patrol enabling them to respond to emergencies more quickly or deterring the incidences altogether. For EMS, it can improve response times that can actually save lives.

Many social and human service agencies and programs need to have the capacity to track the individuals they serve as they move through the system, relocate to other areas, and apply for benefits and services from other agencies. Having a comprehensive view of their beneficiaries can improve the agencies ability to provide the right services to the right people at the right time, reduce the risk of child and sexual abuse, decrease falsification of benefits, and provide a number of other treatments, preventions, and interventions that affect lives. This includes accessing, providing, tracking, and managing the following services.

- Child and infant care
- Disability
- Indigent care
- Welfare
- Education

- Adoption and foster care
- Domestic violence
- Poverty
- Health

- Food safety
- Employment
- Sexual predators

The key to the success in all of these scenarios is to provide agencies with timely and accurate access to the information they need to effectively deliver their services. Since much of this information comes from external sources, it is important to embrace data governance to drive optimal data outcomes. In turn, data governance can help improve the lives, health, and well-being of individuals.

Asset Management

For the purposes of this book, asset management pertains to highly complex scenarios that commonly exist in industries like telecommunications, utilities, or oil and gas. Companies in these fields have a multifaceted array of property such as meters, pipes, towers, circuits, switches, building supplies, valves, compressors, tools, vehicles, cable, generators, portable lights, and other parts and machinery. Managing these assets is equally complex depending upon the number of storage and work locations, as well as the number of employees, contractors, subcontractors, and systems in use.

If assets such as these are not effectively tracked, it will cost a company significant amounts of money in lost materials, project delays, fraud, excessive inventory, and lost depreciation among other things. One of the keys to monitoring these possessions from a physical and financial perspective is to have consistent information to work from. Unfortunately, these industries are prone to data entry errors that come from a variety of sources where employees, contractors, and subcontractors record projects, products, equipment, parts, and worksite information differently. The net result is that assets cannot be efficiently tracked, managed, or accurately depreciated, substantially driving up the cost of doing business.

Take for instance a prominent oil and gas company that decided to automate a portion of their business. For years, their primary contractors had supplied project and work site information using a variety of paper and electronic documents which played havoc with asset management. In order to bring continuity to the process the oil company requested that each of their many contractors submit the information in a new standard electronic format. While each contractor complied, a problem quickly surfaced when the company discovered that each contractor was using different descriptions and codes to describe the same assets. This is clearly a data quality and governance issue that the company will need to resolve.

Certainly oil and gas companies have the financial capacity to address quality and governance issues like these, so why don't they? I can only speculate but it clearly reflects the age-old misconception that technology alone will solve the problem. While technology can automate a number of processes, it is only as good as the data that it has to work with. When it comes to asset management in these environments, data quality and data governance play a crucial role in driving costs down and business performance up.

Business Analytics and Research

Data governance plays a significant role in business analytics and research. At the heart of these disciplines is a need for accurate information that analysts and researchers can leverage to optimize business planning and decision-making. This means having good quality data at the right time and for the right reasons. There are countless ways that organizations use data for research and analytics to drive business. The following represents just a few of these endless examples.

In the government sector agencies are often tasked with researching and providing information at the request of the legislature, council, parliament, governor, prime minister, and president. The accuracy of the research is often scrutinized by the media, the public and opposing political parties. The precision of the research will often determine the course of new and existing programs and laws as well as influence political perceptions for those involved. This type of research and analysis is frequently labor intensive and involves a number of people and resources to complete. A data governance program can help streamline this process and deliver more accurate results.

The insurance and financial field employs actuarial services to assess risk across their businesses. This highly sophisticated profession relies extensively on accurate information from a number of sources in order to project risk and profitability for the company. Actuarial services are a prime beneficiary for a data governance initiative.

Retail businesses have increased their efforts around analytics and research to better prepare and respond to local events and even natural disasters. Based on historical sales, companies look to see what people purchase during special events as well as what they buy in preparation for a hurricane, flood, or snowstorm. The better the information the more profitable the opportunity and the better customer service these organizations can provide.

Higher education depends on research and analytics to track graduates, their post-graduate success, and managing student loans and university endowments. All of which comes together more effectively when data governance has been implemented.

Research and business analytics is used in thousands of ways. Whether an organization is deciding on where to build a new store, lease verses buy, understand the characteristics of its customer base, or how to fight crime, they all require good and timely information to arrive at solid business decisions. Data quality and data governance programs improve these efforts by supplying the accurate information required to make good choices.

Other Business Operations

I have addressed a number of core business operations that derive value from quality and governance initiatives. However, there are many more that are industry specific. Though unique in their own right these business functions have the exact same dependencies for accurate and consistent information to drive their business requirements.

For example, medical device manufacturers and providers must track patients and their implants in order to address recalls and respond to health risks. Likewise, in the pharmaceutical industry data is important for tracking drug trials and supporting research initiatives. For government agencies, it can be about interagency cooperation to thwart benefit fraud, or reduce duplicated administrative and overhead costs.

The point is, that regardless of the circumstances or industry, when it comes to data and information it is about getting it right in support of the business requirement. Doing so brings direct and indirect value to the business in many ways.

Chapter Summary

Data governance and quality programs play an integral role improving any data dependent business function regardless of the industry or business purpose. It does this by driving revenues, decreasing costs, reducing risk, improving compliance, and generating goodwill through customer satisfaction.

The benefit to an organization may not always be visible on the surface but in the end, it can be reasonably justified and quantified. The worth of these programs can be compelling within a single project and even more undeniable when applied across multiple business functions within an organization.

The challenge for most businesses is to understand what is possible and then take the time and effort to examine how information actually impacts core business functions. Driving visibility into these areas of opportunity is sure to reinforce the value and need for quality and governance within any organization.

Chapter 8

Organization Strategy and Policy Value

A mature and well-positioned data governance body will have the wherewithal to establish and manage a number of organization data policies. The visibility this discipline brings should influence organization-wide policies that historically have been left to ad hoc groups, overly controlling individuals, or ignored entirely. While I touched on a few of these topics in earlier chapters, it is important to call them out here, expand upon them, and underscore the importance they have in creating and managing policy and process at an enterprise level.

Customer Definition

Defining a customer, and maintaining that definition and it's metadata across technologies, reports, and business processes, is a common challenge for organizations. For instance, aggregation or reconciliation of multiple reports is a difficult task if each of the reports utilizes a different definition of a customer. I know a number of companies that spend weeks and even months reconciling reports because of this very scenario.

A telecommunications company I once consulted with provides a strong example of this point. The organization's upper management was growing frustrated with their inability to accurately generate reports on critical information across divisions and regions. As a result, executives did not have timely information and lacked trust in the data, and the cost to manually reconcile these reports was excessive.

The crux of the problem was that the company was applying 27 different customer definitions across these reports. One factor contributing to this problem was the company vice presidents who had taken ownership of their own reports and had therefore developed their own definition of a customer. More than anything, the process needed a conductor to step in and develop consistent customer definitions across the company.

For certain organizations it makes perfect sense to have multiple customer definitions, for others a single characterization works just fine. Either way, a data governance body can minimize the number of customer definitions required and centrally manage the application of those definitions across reports, business processes, and technologies.

Merger and Acquisition (M&A)

For some organizations merger and acquisition is a routine part of their business, for others it only comes along once in great while. Regardless, the time and cost of bringing together data from two businesses entities is a costly and rigorous exercise. The technical cost to bring together business transactions and data from separate entities normally represents a sizable portion of the overall investment. What is not measured, and seldom discussed, is the excessive post acquisition cost to fix the data and information problems created during the merger.

Data governance should have a seat at the table and play a significant role in corporate decision making when it comes to mergers and acquisitions. Historically, if there was a chair available it was reserved for IT exclusively. Involving the data governance team lowers pre and post acquisition costs by steering the organization into better short and long-term decisions on data and associated business processes. Furthermore, the group should play an early, proactive role in working with the new entity to standardize data content, formats, processes, and uniting stewardship activities.

Project and Budgetary Planning

The fact that businesses continue to operate in silo environments makes organizational provisions a necessity to ensure data related projects and programs are aligned with corporate interests, best practices, and standards. One way to do this is to require the data governance body to actively participate in all project and budgetary discussions surrounding data and information assets. This proactive approach helps organizations make smarter decisions up front rather than react to them after the fact.

A case in point is that of a data governance program I am very familiar with at a large international company. The stakeholders are very proud of their governance program but are finding themselves in a reactive state nearly 100 percent of the time. The reason is that global projects continue to go forward in vacuums. Once the governance group gets involved, they are faced with the implementation of projects that lack foresight and funding for data quality, business process redesign, data stewardship, and a host of other data centric activities needed to fulfill project expectations. In a few instances, the lack of involvement has even led to the organization's purchase of duplicate or like technologies.

Getting the governance body involved in the project planning and budgeting process is a critical step in proactive global management of your data and information assets.

Technology Selection

The role of technology is obvious and of critical importance. Businesses must have the ability to automate data management functions in order to process high volume transactions, perform complex calculations, store, analyze, and report accurately and timely on the information they collect. Technologies that support these activities are available everywhere and address nearly every business function within an organization.

While technology innovation has lent itself to the proliferation of specialized applications, the results have not always met business expectations. Look at the history of BI, CRM, DW, Data Marts, EDW, MDM, and other data intensive projects. In many instances, one is built on the back of another because its predecessor did not live up to the expectation or demands of the business. In all fairness, the success or lack thereof is not necessarily the fault of any single technology but rather the futile data management practices that organizations choose to carryover from one project to the next. The industry is riddled with horror stories where companies invest millions of dollars into state of the art technology only to find they never really solve their core business problems because they ignored the data.

Nearly all major technology purchases affect the data environment so it is a natural fit to have the data governance group represented in the technology selection process. One reason is that the discipline brings visibility and intellect to the process in a way that mitigates risk, accentuates opportunities, and facilitates business and IT interests. Another basis for their involvement is to prevent or minimize duplication of similar technologies that can drive up the costs associated with software license, hardware, education, training, maintenance, and data management.

I was once involved with a technology firm that had five different data quality technologies within their organization. Only one was associated with merger and acquisition. The other four were the result of decisions made by independent business units. Over time, the company found they had duplicated their software license, education, training, and maintenance costs to the tune of several hundred thousand dollars annually.

The cost was one pain point; the challenge of keeping dedicated and knowledgeable resources for each individual application created an entirely different set of problems. In the end, all but one data quality technology had gone unattended and led to a material degradation of the quality of their data. Having a data governance program that has a hand in technology selection could have averted this problem and subsequent costs.

Another set of technology decisions that warrant data governance involvement is that of Cloud computing and software as a service (SaaS). In both scenarios company data is hosted and/or processed by a third party, which means your organization has even less control over company information and what you can do with it. There are a number of data implications to consider when exploring these solutions and there is no better group to participate in this process than the data governance unit. Every data intensive technology project should include a comprehensive data management strategy that supports the business requirements of the project with the data governance body taking full responsibility for this aspect of the plan.

Data Enrichment

Data enrichment represents activities that augment organizational data with data from other sources, typically from third party service providers. These companies supply data that may contain information on demographics, business-to-business information, industry metrics, financial markets, geographic data, weather, or research information. This information is used to drive a number of business functions within the organization.

While this practice has proven valuable to many organizations, it can be expensive and lead to out of control costs if it goes unregulated within the enterprise. Excessive data enrichment costs are more common than one might think and stem from two primary culprits: duplicated services and poor data quality.

Data enrichment services are typically implemented for a specific business purpose and often under the direction of an individual business unit. This silo approach often leaves organizations paying for the same data service in more than one location in the organization. In some cases it is not warranted while in other cases it may be justified. An organization needs to have visibility and control into all data enrichment services in order to minimize duplicated services and better leverage their purchasing power with data suppliers.

A data quality program is essential for optimizing any data enrichment project. In order to accomplish the task of matching third party data with organization data, the information within the organization must be as accurate as possible. Keep in mind that service providers often charge for every record the company sends the provider for processing, which means companies end up paying needlessly for records that do not match or records that match but are duplicated within the corporate database. Accurate internal data results in better third party matches, lower costs, and optimization of the data for business purposes.

I once worked with a company that spent $4 million annually subscribing to nearly 40 data enrichment services. It was not until the organization sanctioned an inventory of these practices that they began to understand the full extent and costs associated with these data services. Their research found that approximately 15 percent of the services were being duplicated or had become obsolete to business operations and could be eliminated. While I am not aware of the final outcome, the organization was expecting to reduce their costs by nearly $1 million dollars annually by incorporating a data governance and data quality program, reducing duplication of service, and re-negotiating with providers.

A common source of excessive data enrichment can be found in marketing programs where campaign data is augmented through external sources. One case that stands out in my mind is the work I did for the marketing arm of a technology company. The organization was sending their consumer data to two different data providers every month in order to augment a number of demographics. This was an automated process where consumer data was sent to the first data provider and when returned, the augmented data was forwarded to the second provider.

Upon inspection, I learned that there were no provisions for data quality and no manual intervention took place until data had been passed through both service providers. It was also determined that approximately 15 percent of the records sent out were duplicates, this corresponded to increased costs in the range of 12-15 percent. In addition, another 4-5 percent of the records sent out for processing came back with no match because key data elements were either missing or incorrect. The negative impact of this process and the poor quality of the data from start to finish was estimated to have cost the company hundreds of thousands of dollars annually.

Data governance programs allow organizations to drive visibility into areas such as data enrichment that are normally off limits to traditional management structures. This involvement inevitably leads to better results and lower costs to the organization.

Other Areas for Corporate Involvement

While we covered a number of areas of opportunity in previous chapters, it is critical to underscore the importance of integrating data governance into the following processes and at a corporate level.

- Data security and privacy
- Risk and compliance
- Business partner integration

In doing so organizations will optimize the unique value this practice has to offer.

Chapter Summary

The beauty of a mature data governance program is that it brings the right minds together under a shared cause. The value this discipline can bring to corporate/agency strategy and policy is immeasurable. High performance organizations will look beyond the bits and bytes of traditional, tactical data governance and leverage the intellectual property of this domain for the greater good of the business.

Chapter 9

Organizational Structure and Alignment

At this point, you might be thinking that data governance is something your company may want to explore further but you have reservations and several questions. A common question I hear is, "how can something as complex and dynamic as data governance be constructed in a way that is both effective and cost conscious?" Furthermore, how is this accomplished on a large or global scale? Before we dive into the how let's first examine the basic requirements of a successful data governance organization structure. Keep in mind that these essential requirements apply to data governance programs of all shapes, size, and complexity.

Foundational Requirements for a Successful Data Governance Organization Structure

Legitimacy

A data governance program must be formally sanctioned, endorsed, and a recognized discipline within the organization. I have witnessed too many organizations implement their data governance program as an extension of an existing function; consequently, the data governance program becomes buried in the day-to-day bureaucracy. While there are many reasons for this, it is usually because the data governance program inherits the limitations and baggage of its parent function, such as limited authority, funding, and visibility. Extending legitimacy to the program means that everyone in the organization needs to recognize the data governance discipline and its leadership.

Span of Control over Data

Data governance must be empowered with formal authority and accountability over corporate information and data assets that span all lines of business. This reinforces the notion that data is a corporate asset and not the property of a sole business unit. It also empowers the discipline to pursue areas of opportunity for the company that would normally be off limits. This said, there are also reasonable exceptions to the rule.

The most notable exception is financial information as it pertains to the traditional general ledger, chart of accounts, accounts receivable, payroll, and other core financial systems. For most companies these processes are a staple to running the business and have been governed and regulated for some time both internally and externally. While there are aspects of financial data that are worth looking into on a project-by-project basis, the governance of financial systems in general should remain with the financial arm of the organization.

Other possible exceptions, or at least partial exceptions to this rule, could pertain to data and systems managed by human resources, medical records, and/or the legal arm of the organization. Due to the nature, specialization, and confidentiality of the data it may be sensible for certain groups to retain a higher level of ownership rights to their data. However, these same groups should be represented within the framework of the data governance organization in order to help facilitate cross-functional opportunities for the organization.

For practical reasons organizations also should consider a stair-step approach in exercising their span of control for data. The program may start with an initial focus such as a project; however, the data governance organization should be empowered to expand their reach at their discretion and for the right business reasons in the future. Organizations that do not clearly establish their short and long-term span of control for this program find themselves struggling at some point to engage the various lines of business and act on opportunities when they arise.

Span of Control over Data Process

The governance program must have the authority to define, implement, and enforce data processes, roles, and responsibilities across lines of business that support the collective data management initiative. In other words, get people to play nice in the sandbox. The very nature of this discipline requires people to work in unison and that will not happen if the program operates on a volunteer or opt-out basis. Obviously, this should be completed with the full participation of everyone involved. At the same time, it cannot be perceived as a volunteer exercise in futility.

For most businesses, the span of control for data process is about organizing and coordinating existing resources that are already performing some level of data management activities and getting them to follow common processes. This simply gives the data governance body the authority to align data related activities performed by people across the organization.

I equate this to the same level of authority that the finance department has over financial policy, process, and procedures within a business. Few people actually report directly to the financial business unit, yet the expectation to follow the policies and procedures set forth by the finance division persists throughout the organization. The same should hold true for data governance.

Funding

Yes, it does require a modest initial investment to launch a data governance program. It also has ongoing costs associated with it and that can be fully justified based on the business value the program delivers. However, the investment may not be as involved as you think. Keep in mind that the majority of this program is about coordinating and repurposing existing resources and activities that the organization is already performing. At the same time, an underfunded program is doomed to fail. I have seen plenty of examples in the industry that would support this argument.

Administrative Visibility

Few other programs span the business, political, and cultural boundaries in an organization in the way that data governance does. Because of this, the program must have high-level sponsorship and visibility. Positioning the program deep in the bowels of the organization creates an out-of-sight, out-of-mind scenario that is sure to stunt the best of intentions. The discipline needs to operate at a level within the organization that has universal recognition.

Senior Management Involvement

Don't panic! Senior management will not need to immerse themselves into the tactical, day-to-day data governance operations, or be paraded through an endless array of meetings. Senior management does need to assist in navigating political waters, aligning business units, providing top-level issue resolution, underscoring the value of the program, and enabling the office of data governance to perform their operational duties.

There are a number of creative ways to integrate upper management into this process that do not require significant investments of time and resources. At the same time, upper level management does need to be committed to the cause.

Skill & Position

The people that lead data governance programs must have a strong mix of administrative, technical, business, and leadership skills. Leaders must be positioned in the organizational hierarchy such that they command the attention and respect from others in the company. Unfortunately, I have witnessed situations where organizations take a staff-level or technical focused person with limited leadership and administration skills and asked them to lead a data governance program, which they were ill equipped to guide. On the flipside, I also have seen organizations appoint well-qualified people to lead these programs without the appropriate position or title in the company to be successful.

Aptitude, title, and position can be a differentiator between success and failure.

Data governance programs must be self-sustaining structures to weather the changes that come with corporate reorganization, project completion, economic downturn, and cultural or political events. The more organizations can do to satisfy these basic requirements, the better positioned they are to become self-sustaining, successful, and a value-add program within the business.

Foundational Structure

Every organizational structure is different. This is not a bad thing, but like anything else, some work better than others do. What I present here are concepts for organizational structures that complement the foundational requirements for a successful data governance program. These concepts can be scaled up or down to suit the needs of the company or agency. There are equally diverse methods for implementing these models.

The important point to take away from this section is how the organizational structure satisfied foundational requirements for success. The organizational charts themselves are secondary. The closer organizations can come to implementing these concepts the more successful they are likely to be. Organizations that venture away from these concepts expose their data governance programs to greater risk.

The Triple Indemnity Model

The triple indemnity model (Figure 9.1) for data governance architecture is by far the most sound given that it satisfies each of the structural requirements for a successful data governance organization. It does this by incorporating a triple layer of insurance for success that comes in the form of an office, council, and a wildcard. When implemented together they make for a very strong, effective, and sustainable governance program.

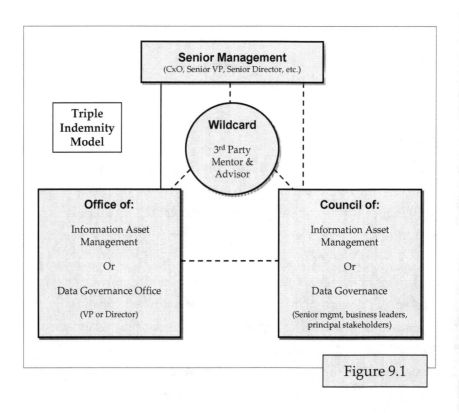

Figure 9.1

1) **Office of Information Asset Management or Data Governance** – Establishing a formal "office" to manage the company's information assets satisfies a few key requirements for successful data governance. First, is satisfies the need to certify the program as a formal discipline within the company that people and lines of business recognize and have to deal with. Second, it satisfies administrative visibility by reporting into senior management. Last, conveying the appropriate authority to this office also provides the span of control it needs over data and process to be successful.

   The office is responsible for daily operations and depending on the size of the organization, the person leading the department should be a vice president or director level position. In most cases, this is not a job for a staff employee, unless they are qualified to perform at a senior manager level.

2) **Information Asset Management or Data Governance Council** – The purpose of the council is to enable the office to be successful. Some people will ask, "Why can't the office do this on their own if I give them everything they need?" While this is a legitimate question, the reality of the situation is that this discipline finds itself on the front lines of more political and cultural wars than perhaps any other corporate discipline. The council helps the office navigate these barriers and facilitate organizational alignment and change management across these lines of demarcation. The council also raises visibility within upper management and

assists the office with securing funding and support for their initiatives going forward. Collectively the council reinforces the company's ability to satisfy every requirement for a successful structure.

3) **Wildcard** – The wildcard represents a third party change agent, mentor, and advisor that can assist the organization in any number of capacities that may be the difference between success and failure. A qualified wildcard should be able to help steer the organization in the right direction by providing business acumen, sound best practices, industry insight, thought leadership, advocacy, experience, and play the good cop/bad cop role as needed. The good thing about a wildcard is this does not have to be a full-time role and it can be effectively leveraged at the appropriate times.

Often times, individuals within an organization are too close to a situation to progress past problems. I have observed this countless times over the years even when the individuals are highly qualified and tenured. The best-laid plans can quickly succumb to personal agendas and there is no better example of this than what takes place in the data governance space on a routine basis. A wildcard can mitigate these risks as well as supplement the skills within the organization that are either missing or need honing. Similar to the council, the wildcard adds insurance for success by helping the company satisfy a number of foundational structure requirements.

Staffing & Reporting Structures

The Office

The question inevitably arises as to whom the office should report to. There is no single answer to this question. What I will say is that information asset management is a function of the business, which also has unique interdependencies on IT. I am of the mindset that the office should report into the business and not an IT department. Maintaining the office under IT also perpetuates an unhealthy impression that IT owns the data when it is not an exclusive IT asset.

From my perspective, the best choice is to have the office report into the finance division and the chief financial officer. There are some very good reasons for this. One is that finance is more agnostic and far less political than most parts of the organization. Another is that this business unit has clout across the enterprise and not just in a single domain within the business. Yet another is that finance has the mindset of what it takes to mange assets across the continuum of the enterprise because that is what they do with financial assets. Finally, if a data governance program effectively demonstrates their value to the financial arm of the company they are far more likely to receive the funding and support they need going forward.

The next question commonly asked is, "who and what reports into the office?" This too will vary from one organization to the next and will likely change over time as the program matures. One thing is clear; the office should have three lines of reporting: direct and indirect reporting of individuals and direct functional reporting of groups and committees. In addition, the office should have membership responsibilities to certain existing committees and task forces within the company (Figure 9.2).

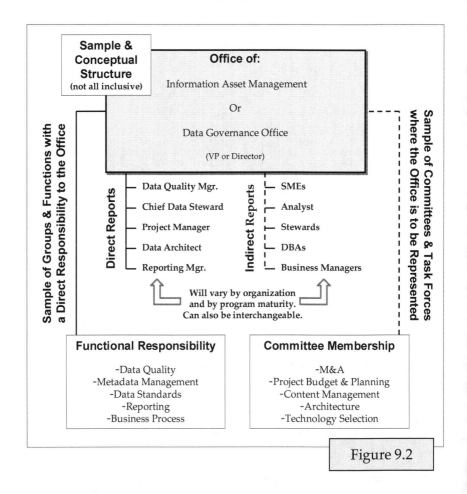

Figure 9.2

In the beginning, most organizations have very few if any direct reports into the office. Most start with individuals and groups assuming a dotted line responsibility to the office. Certain roles will gradually transition under the direction of the office when it makes sense functionally and organizationally. One starting model that seems to be gaining quick acceptance is where the office originates with a lead individual and a small team of data quality specialists reporting directly to them.

For example, data quality specialists may already exist within the IT department and moving them into the office as direct reports may be a natural fit. On the other hand, data stewards may be a collection of analysts and SME's from various departments that have a full or part-time role in data management. They are likely to continue as direct reports into their home department but will have specific responsibilities for the data as outlined by the office. In this case, they would be considered indirect reports with functional responsibilities to the office.

At some point, it may make sense to bring certain roles into the office so that their skills and expertise can be leveraged across the broader organization. In other words, create a Center of Excellence where core intellectual property and subject matter expertise is leveraged to the benefit of all projects. Such an arrangement can cover domain expertise in the areas of quality, reporting, project management, metadata management, stewardship, data architecture, and more.

The Council

The council should be staffed by no more than eight people under the principal that "eight or less is best." Larger groups do not have a track record for making effective and timely decisions. One position should be reserved for the person who leads the office; one for a lead technology representative such as the CIO, the remainder should be filled by upper management representing a cross-section of the company business. It may make sense to rotate certain members given the focus of the program at any point in time. The great thing about the council concept is that it requires a small commitment of time and no other real investment. It is almost like taking out free insurance on your data governance program.

In practice, the council agenda is prepared by the leader of the office with nothing coming to the attention of this team unless it is in need of action or strategic corporate direction. This means the group may need to meet a couple times per month in the beginning and then scale back their involvement as the program matures. In reality, the council can evolve from a bi-weekly to a monthly or even quarterly meeting format. As the office concept matures, the council may be able to dissolve entirely.

Another recommendation is not to adopt a consensus model for this committee or any other group that is formed under the data governance program. Consensus will simply paralyze the entire process. Simple models where the majority rules among those in attendance will keep people actively engaged and prevent the process from stalling. If necessary, a proxy system can serve as a viable option to consensus.

Special Interest Groups

Another important structural consideration pertains to how the office interfaces with various interest groups that may have overlapping or complementary roles and responsibilities. Like any other initiative of this magnitude, it can create a backlash of concern from people, groups, committees, and business units that may already be performing some of these duties today. Common examples of groups that come into play under these circumstances include teams and committees that represent:

- Architecture
- Project planning and budgeting (MDM, CRM, BI, DW, EDW, ERP, CDI, etc.)
- Data quality
- Data standards
- Merger and acquisition
- Content management
- Records management
- Business process management
- Internal audit

The goal of this exercise is not to disband existing groups and their initiatives, but rather to explore how they can be integrated into the data governance process and vice versa. Some situations may require dissolving an existing group and rolling its function into the data governance office. In others, it may align existing groups to assume a dotted line responsibility to the data governance office. Yet in other cases it may dictate that the leader of the data governance office have a seat on pre-existing and future committees. Over time each of these relationships can and will change as the office and the program matures.

As an example, a pre-existing team developing data standards should come under the direction of the office. On the other hand, project teams that are planning, budgeting, and implementing data intensive projects (i.e., MDM, CRM, BI, DW, data migration, etc.) will need to include the office lead as part of their active committee membership. Each instance supports the fundamental requirement for span of control for data and process by involving the office lead directly or indirectly into data activities of the organization.

Chapter Summary

Every data governance program exists at a unique place in the organizational structure, even when compared to others in the same industry. The objective when designing a structure is not to emulate that of another organization, nor to be overly concerned with reporting hierarchies. First and foremost, the objective is to establish a structure that satisfies, to the extent possible, the foundational requirements for a successful data governance structure. Once this is accomplished, it is much easier to fill in the pieces and define reporting structures, roles, and responsibilities.

Data governance programs mature over time. While there are certain structural concepts that are important and should be embraced on day one, the precise makeup of the program should be expected to grow and evolve over time. The more an organization can satisfy the foundational requirements for a successful data governance structure the better they position themselves for growth, self-sustainment, and success.

Chapter 10

Technology

Technology plays a vital role in data governance by automating data policy established through the business process. The importance of technology is such that data governance frequently prompts organizations to evaluate their existing technology portfolio in support of the governance initiative. After all, organizations must have data governance enabled tools that are sufficiently robust to implement complex data policies, business rules, and data management work flows.

Several technologies claim to automate the facilitation of data governance policy. Like any software application, some perform very well in this space while others fall short of expectations. The one certainty is that none of these purported technologies can

---

possibly automate every process for governing data; rather, it is a combination of tools that support the overall effort.

This chapter is not intended to make technology decisions for you; however, it is important to understand which technologies are involved and how they contribute to the automation of data policy and overall data management.

Common Data Governance Technologies

Several technologies exist today that perform some level of data governance automation. These technologies can reside at the integration and application layers and may come in the form of specialized tools, core business applications, and various integration solutions. The most common technologies associated with the data governance space involve the following:

Data Integration Technologies

Data integration represents the assimilation tools that are responsible for accessing and moving data between systems. While their primary purpose is to access and move information between data sources, these tools also invoke a number of data transformation processes as data passes between systems.

The sophistication of data integration tools has grown over the years with the development of specialized adapters, connectors, drivers, and imbedded processes such as data quality and extract, transform, and load (ETL). These tools also have been refined and tuned to move data bi-directionally and in high volume batch and real-time environments.

Data integration tools must have the technical capacity to access and move data within complex heterogeneous environments, as well as automate sophisticated data governance policies within the workflow itself. As organizations evaluate these capabilities it is important to consider how data integration tools can be leveraged across the broader organization and future projects, not just to fulfill an immediate need.

Data Quality Technologies

Data quality represents tools that perform data parsing, cleansing, standardization, enrichment, linking, and consolidation of data. This is a mission-critical technology that is at the core of automating data quality operations in high volume environments. The application of these tools is essential for the success of data intensive projects.

Data quality tools have been around for several years, beginning first with the development of address correction software. While an address remains an important component to data quality, the technologies have expanded to other data domains such as name, product, parts, personal information, and entity. In addition, these tools often deal with sophisticated record matching and operate in a variety of batch and real-time settings for both B2B and B2C environments.

At their core, data quality technologies should be business rule based in order to implement complex data governance policies that are inevitable with data quality solutions. Organizations evaluating data quality tools also should consider the tool's ability to scale over time and deal with multiple data domains, international data, batch, and real-time integration into multiple disparate systems.

Data Profile Technologies

Data profile technologies represent analytic tools that inspect, monitor, and report on the condition of the data. These tools are often used by SMEs, DBAs, and business analysts to proactively examine, fix, and report on data anomalies. Profiling applications help organizations move from a reactive to a proactive state by understanding the condition of data in quantifiable terms.

Profiling tools are extremely useful and cost effective. They are useful in the sense that organizations can quickly identify and quantify the condition of their data. The tools are cost effective in the sense that they do not require extensive coding and maintenance of SQL scripts and reports to generate the desired output. For this reason they can be used by both technologist and some members of the business community. Profiling technologies are applied to data migration work, inspecting and quantifying the condition of data for the first time, monitoring and trending data outcomes over time, and analyzing data in order to understand unique and often hidden relationships between transactions and events.

Like other data governance technologies, the strength of the profile tool will reside in its ability to incorporate complex data governance policy into the software. One word of caution when evaluating data profile tools is to take into consideration the skill set of the people that will be using the application. Most robust profile tools are geared towards technical or power users on the business side and are too sophisticated for the everyday business user.

Data Remediation and Work Flow Management Technologies

Data remediation and workflow management represent the emerging technologies that deal with the automation of documentation, data exception handling, and decision-making workflows associated with data governance. Technology supports many data related processes; but, it does not solve every data anomaly that falls outside of automated thresholds nor does it facilitate every decision. I underscore the point that this is an emerging set of tools because most technologies today lag behind in developing and implementing workflows that support these aspects of the data governance process.

Workflow and remediation capabilities are beginning to take shape within some of the technologies noted in this chapter but it remains an immature market. Because of this, many organizations are faced with costly manual processes just to document and handle data exceptions and arbitrary decision making that go with managing data.

Organizations evaluating data governance enabled technologies should look closely at the ability of the tools to remediate, delegate, and escalate anomalies and circumstances that fall outside of thresholds, routine processes, and automation capabilities. Otherwise, having to manually deal with documentation, process flow, and exceptions can be a costly venture.

Master Data Management Technologies

Master Data Management (MDM) represents technologies that manage, link, and synchronize mission-critical data elements across disparate systems in a way that reflects a single or holistic view of the business. MDM is a highly sophisticated solution and comes in multiple forms. In any case, it requires well-defined data policies on what constitutes a master record and the workflows that support it. These rules involve a myriad of decision rights related to data survivorship, consolidation, systems of record, transformation, data ownership, data unification, and escalation.

Technologies that support MDM must be able to accommodate complex data governance policies and procedures developed through the data governance business process. In fact, MDM solutions are possibly more reliant on data governance enabled technologies and processes than any other data centric solution.

Data Modeling Technologies

Data modeling tools represent technologies that support the development and maintenance of an organization's physical and logical data models. These tools help IT professionals implement and manage a number of data governance policies within the data architecture. This includes how data is structured, formatted, referenced, accessed, and stored within databases and information systems.

A clearly defined and common data model significantly reduces ongoing development, integration, and maintenance costs within IT. Data modeling technology helps to effectively implement data governance policies at an architecture level.

Metadata Management Technologies

Metadata management technologies represent tools that can store and manage metadata from a central location where changes are propagated out to all dependent objects and systems. Central repository structures such as this make it possible to manage intricate metadata environments and at far less cost.

While the industry is making inroads into comprehensive metadata management tools that span multiple applications, the reality is that most metadata management capabilities are restricted by application. As organizations evaluate data governance technologies it is important to appraise the technology's ability to store, manage, and share metadata within their environment.

Additional Technologies and Considerations

There are a host of additional technologies that entities leverage in the data governance arena, including those that cover data lineage, security, and data stewardship solutions. The important thing to remember about these and other tools is for organizations to raise the questions around their ability to effectively implement data governance policy and associated work flows that go with it.

As mentioned earlier, this book was not written to make your technology decisions for you. We could debate the entire list of variables: build vs. buy; feature vs. function; stack vs. best of breed; price vs. value; total cost of ownership; innovation vs. big brother; and more. I will leave the decision-making up to the reader. Nevertheless, here are a few additional considerations for organizations evaluating data governance technologies.

Cloud Software and Software as a Service (SaaS)

The industry is moving towards more Cloud and SaaS based solutions where data is hosted by a third party. While this may be an attractive cost reduction proposition for organizations these same entities must be prepared to give up more control of their data if they elect to go down this path. By giving up more control they further limit their ability to govern their own information.

An example of this is the organization that invested large amounts of money over several years into their CRM system. Part of this investment included real-time verification of existing customers so that as new records were added, duplicate customer records were prevented from entering the database. The company switched to a Cloud based system from another vendor and lost all control over their ability to validate and prevent the duplication of records at point of entry, which has negatively impacted their business across the board.

Organizations need to examine their capabilities for governing and managing their data under Cloud and SaaS models and weigh the cost/benefit from it. Furthermore, companies and agencies that pursue these solutions need to help suppliers of these technologies pursue innovative ways to govern data in these environments.

International Capability

The world has grown much smaller as more and more organizations conduct business across international boundaries. The globalization of business is attributed largely to the advent of the Internet and applies to traditional domestic businesses as well as those with physical worldwide operations.

International business operations push the envelope for data management and governance. These challenges present a horde of logical and technical issues: language translation; single and double byte character processing; regionalization of names; individual country addressing systems; culture; timing of information; and much more.

Data governance enabled technologies need to have the capacity to handle a large number of international data requirements. At the same time, keep in mind that no technology or combination of technologies comes close to handling every characteristic and requirement of international data. Organizations will need to evaluate their international requirements very closely and focus on those aspects of the data that make the most business sense.

Real-Time, Batch, Near Real Time Capabilities

Data governance technologies must be able to operate within various real-time, near real-time, and batch environments. While the purpose for this is largely self-evident (quick access to current information), the most overlooked reason for these capabilities has to do with the data life cycle.

The data life cycle often crosses scores of systems, databases, and processes. The technologies that govern data must be able to operate instantaneously and consistently within and between each of these systems. This includes related upstream and downstream processes and systems that influence data outcomes. Having the capacity to operate within one system but not another creates inconsistent data outcomes and overall problems with data management and data integrity.

A prime example of this is data quality technologies. Data quality technologies must be able to perform a number of validation, standardization, and harmonization procedures at all points where data enters, moves, is stored, and consumed within the data life cycle. This means having the ability to call these procedures within a number of real-time and batch processes and within and between a number of heterogeneous systems.

Organizations evaluating data governance technologies should consider the capacity of these tools to address current and future needs across the entire data life cycle and enterprise.

Chapter Summary

There are a number of things to take into consideration when evaluating data governance enabling technologies. The first is to accept the notion that no single technology can automate every data governance policy or work flow, and that it takes a combination of tools to accomplish this. Second, is to understand the portfolio of tools that is required to attain effective data governance. Lastly, it is to understand some of the capabilities and risks to consider when evaluating technologies, and how they effectively address the full data life cycle.

Chapter 11

Measuring Performance

Performance metrics for data governance programs are evolving with the discipline itself. The dynamic nature of the discipline has left many organizations unsure about which metrics to track and how they can be quantified. This uncertainty is further compounded by the fact that many of the business benefits provided by data governance cannot be expressed in neat economic terms. This is disconcerting given that the future of the entire data governance program is often dependent upon its ability to demonstrate value and purpose for the organization.

A simple solution is to focus performance measurement around the activities known to drive value, as discussed in Chapters 3-8.

That said, there are a number of creative techniques that can be leveraged to accomplish this. Some methods use traditional means whereas others clearly unconventional, but are no less effective. When you put them all together, it creates a compelling set of metrics for measuring performance and elevating visibility for the program.

Five Ways to Measure Performance

There are several ways to measure data governance performance but most will fall into one of five categories.

- Business performance using data metrics
- Risk and compliance
- Data management operations
- Miscellaneous business operations
- Transparency log

When recording performance within these categories data governance leadership needs to take into account opportunities, events, projects, and actions that the discipline influences and summarize it in a way that business leaders can appreciate. This should obviously include the financial impact as well as the level of influence the data governance process has on bringing transparency and visibility to the problem.

1) Business Performance Using Data Metrics

The most pervasive industry practice for measuring data governance and quality performance is to measure business performance against data outcomes. It traditionally involves measuring data against benchmark metrics and then relating it back to business performance improvement. The foundation for these performance metrics is the operational data and the business case it supports.

The practice of measuring data involves the utilization of data profile and quality technologies to determine the starting condition of the data, correct the data, and then monitor and respond to changes over time. The results are recorded and summarized into reports that reflect the level of success data governance has achieved in regard to data quality.

For example, a manufacturing company that has part number errors within their product database conducts an initial data profile and finds that 23 percent of their part numbers are incorrect. The inaccurate parts can be further broken down into a number of categories that better reflect the nature of the problem. These categories include invalid format, null value, non-numeric, and so forth. Correcting the data and implementing data governance policy enables the company to reduce and maintain the number of incorrect part numbers at 3 percent. The company can conclude that the data governance program improved the condition of the data by 20 percent.

The next step for the manufacturing company is to tie the 20 percent data improvement to cost reduction estimates reflected in the business case or in actual manufacturing performance. If the business case estimated a reduction in manufacturing costs of $50,000 annually for every 5 percent improvement in parts information then it would be safe to say that the program lowered costs by $200,000 per year. On the other hand, if the actual cost impact associated with reducing manufacturing delays and inventory control becomes known, then this would be the better measurement to use.

There are two extremely important assumptions with the previous example. The first is that the organization actually completed a business case for the program and it was sufficient enough to reasonably and accurately estimate the financial effect of the program. The second assumption is that the organization actually went back to measure results against the business case and/or real business performance. Unfortunately, most organizations do neither of these.

An alarming number of organizations start data governance programs without a business case, or a weak one at best. In these instances, the data metrics that are produced from these programs have no meaning to business people because the data itself shows little relevance to business performance. For businesses that do complete a business case, they seldom go back and tie data outcomes to it. One reason is if the business case is weak to begin with, it is nearly impossible to derive the value added from the data outcomes. Organizational culture can be another reason as many take the time to justify the expenditure initially, but seldom go back and evaluate the program or project performance. When was the last time your organization went back to measure the business impact a project really had when it comes to MDM, BI, CRM, EDW, DW, ERP, and so on?

Too many organizations have yet to build the bridge that connects data metrics to business outcomes. Data metrics are an important aspect of measuring data governance performance but raw data alone is not going to sustain a data governance program. Organizations need to make sure they are taking the appropriate steps to translate data improvements into business benefit.

2) Risk & Compliance

This category for performance measurement represents events and actions taken by the data governance group that directly influence risk and compliance. Though operational data may be used, measurements in this category are rarely based on pure data metrics. To the contrary, risk and compliance performance is more frequently measured financially against events, projects, probability outcomes, and in some cases year-over-year financial improvements.

One of the biggest drivers for data governance comes from organization risk and compliance. For industries like financial services and insurance, it is at the core of their business model. Minimizing risk and improving compliance can have a major impact on business performance so it is only natural that data governance programs call out and measure their influence in these areas.

Tangible improvements in risk and compliance obviously need documentation. This often is accomplished through a noted reduction in year-over-year fines, fees, audits, losses, and other costly events tied to these activities. The bigger challenge with risk and compliance endeavors is that they are seldom tied directly to data metrics or the bottom line of the business. Many organizations do not give adequate consideration to risk or non-compliance unless an incident arises. This should not discourage a data governance organization from measuring performance in this area.

All events and actions taken to minimize risk and improve compliance can be recorded through a log, even the intangible ones. For example:

Entry Number: #9

Date: 5/21/2011

Opportunity: Reduce fraudulent and accidental overpayment of sales commissions.

Event: Sales notified the data governance committee of fraudulent activities involving a sales partner costing the company approximately $85,000 over a six-month period. In addition, the data integrity difficulties within the database are assumed to be contributing to overpayment of an unspecified amount in sales commissions.

Actions: Implement data quality and data governance measures across the sales management databases. These new measures alert sales management of possible inconsistencies between sales orders from partners and captive agents, and the associated transactions related to invoices, product, shipments, returns, and possible duplicate customer orders. These actions are expected to reduce the overall risk of fraud and accidental overpayment of sales commissions.

Financial Impact: Reasonable, conservative estimate of $200,000 in annual cost savings based on both the one-time $85,000 fraudulent loss and overpayment examples shared by sales management. This estimate is supported by auditors, sales management, and analysts involved.

Transparency Impact: None, the risk was known to the organization. However, data governance body provided the mechanism to create and deliver a solution.

Obviously, if risk and compliance can be tangibly measured in financial terms then the organization should clearly report the figures. For actions that have no measurable impact it is advisable to get a number of influential people and groups like the council to support a "reasonable" financial number, based on experiences, that reflects cost savings or cost avoidance. If generating a figure is simply out of the question than note that the risk or non-compliance is a non-event until it happens and that the actions of the data governance group have a material effect on keeping it from ever happening.

The risk and compliance log should reflect data governance actions that are material in nature, even if the cost savings or cost avoidance cannot be tangibly justified. The collective notation of these events and actions help reflect the performance of the data governance body and the influence it has on overall risk and compliance.

3) Data Management Operations

Performance measurement represents efficiencies achieved in data management operations that lead to tangible and intangible cost reductions. This is typically measured in the financial gains provided by various events or projects, rather than operational data metrics. The impact data governance has on these operations cannot be measured through data metrics and some cannot be measured at all. However, the influence data governance has on data management operations is significant and should be recorded as part of the performance metrics of the program. For example:

Entry Number: #12

Date: 6/19/2011

Opportunity: Avoid the cost of hiring an approved and budgeted position in department ABC for the purpose of profiling and analyzing data with the XYZ database. Instead, absorb this activity within the framework of the existing Center of Excellence for data stewardship.

Event: Brought to the attention of the data governance council during the meeting on 6/19/2011 by a council member with knowledge of the budgeted position.

Actions: Profile and monitoring activities were started for department ABC by the data stewardship program on 6/30/2011.

Financial Impact: $50,000 in annual cost avoidance.

Transparency Impact: Knowledge of this situation would not have been visible to the company or appropriate actions taken in a business-as-usual environment.

4) Miscellaneous Business Operations

Miscellaneous business operations are a catchall for recording business performance in areas that do not fall into either of the other categories. These performance metrics commonly come from events, projects, and actions taken by the data governance group rather than from pure operational data metrics.

There are a number of additional business operations that are positively influenced by data governance and that fall outside the previously defined categories. Like those noted above these events, actions, and results also should be attributed to the performance of the data governance program. For example:

Entry Number: #5

Date: 6/30/2011

Opportunity: Avoid costs associated with duplication of similar technology

Event: The North American marketing organization requested to purchase from an approved budget similar but different data quality and profile technologies than what are currently in use across world-wide operations. The estimated first year cost of the software license, implementation, education, and maintenance was $650,000. Ongoing costs for software maintenance and internal technical support is estimated at $100,000 annually.

Actions: The data governance organization became involved and alerted the North American group to existing technologies and intellectual capital available to solve their quality problems from within the organization. North America marketing has since implemented the technology from the existing provider and embraced the support of the data governance organization.

Financial Impact: One time cost savings of $400,000 and $75,000 annual cost avoidance after extending existing software license. In addition, it leaves the company with a single suite of products to support.

Transparency Impact: Knowledge of this situation may or may not have been visible to the company. However, the influence of the data governance group or any other group in this situation could not have occurred in a business-as-usual environment.

5) Transparency Log

In my mind, transparency remains the single greatest gift a data governance program can give an organization. It creates a lucid environment that gives way to hidden and even unthinkable opportunities. Given the magnitude of this data governance benefit, it too should be measured.

As indicated in previous performance measurement examples the role data governance plays in driving transparency and visibility must to be recorded for every type of opportunity. These occurrences need to be summarized in a transparency log where business leaders can easily see the impact data governance has on driving corporate transparency and how it leads to improved business performance.

These lucid events need to be restricted to opportunities that are material in nature and would never have been discovered in a business-as-usual environment. The idea is not to create a list of every translucent moment possible but rather those that clearly have a noteworthy impact on the organization.

Each of these five categories needs to be summarized in reports and presented in a way senior management, business leaders, and program participants can understand and appreciate. Collectively, they serve as a powerful mechanism for demonstrating improvements in business performance and justifying the existence of a data governance program.

Chapter Summary

The key for measuring data governance performance is to first acknowledge that it cannot possibly be calculated on data alone. Furthermore, businesses must also be willing to accept the fact that not every benefit generated from a governance program can be tangibly measured. Connecting data metrics to business performance is essential. However, organizations must also recognize the benefits and value data governance generates from the actions, transparency, and events it initiates.

By measuring data governance within the five categories presented in this chapter, organizations can begin to paint a holistic view of their data governance performance and the positive influence this dynamic discipline has on the overall business.

Chapter 12

Getting Started

Where and how you start on the road to information asset management has a lot to do with where your company or institution is at today, your immediate requirements, your appetite for change, internal skill sets, and your budget. Regardless, more than likely there is a solution out there that fits the requirements of your specific organization. Here are a couple things to consider as you venture down the path of data governance.

Find a Mentor and Advisor

The sheer nature of data governance combined with its history of success and failure warrants that organizations seriously consider engaging a qualified third party to serve as an advisor and mentor. Now this may seem self serving coming from the mouth of someone who happens to be a consultant, but the fact of the matter is that mentors really do help organizations excel. A third party can be particularly useful in helping to identify best practices, map strategies, design structures, define business value, align business and IT interests, find opportunities, drive awareness, and cut through the politics that go with the territory. In the end a good, experienced consultant working in this capacity can help an organization save money and rapidly position the program for success.

I am not suggesting for a moment that you need a team of consultants to come in and complete all the work for you. In fact, I'd recommend that organizations do as much of the work as possible for themselves. After all, data governance is a discipline that needs to be woven into the fabric of the organization.

What I am saying is that at minimum, businesses should consider hiring an experienced consultant early in the process to serve in an advisory capacity for the purpose of building the program. The level of involvement this person has in the program may be near full-time in the early stages but should transition to an ad hoc role as the program matures. Additionally, leveraging this advocacy role in the post implementation period is a great way to add insurance, sustainability, and growth. This low cost, high value model is something organizations should seriously consider as they wade into the waters of data governance.

Conduct an Information Asset Management Assessment

Conduct an information asset management assessment to examine, quantify, and validate the state of the company data and the information management ecosystem it resides in. Such an assessment should focus at minimum on the:

- Primary business drivers for the program and/or project
- Quality and timeliness of the data and information in support of the business drivers
- Data elements impacting quality outcomes
- Business processes that impact data and informational outcomes
- Technologies and system integration that impacts data and informational outcomes
- Current lines of data ownership, roles, and responsibilities
- Lines of business, committees, and interest groups involved and level of involvement
- People and positions involved
- Principal data management activities associated with the initial program
- Economic impact

Basically, the deliverables for an assessment should be to identify and quantify the value, material challenges, opportunities, and risk associated with the data and information management environment. This is a very useful exercise. More than anything it brings clarity and visibility into the problem and opportunities and helps organizations begin to focus their attention in the right areas and for the right reasons. It also serves as a solid foundation in support of a business case.

Build a Business Case

As mentioned earlier, the importance of a business case cannot be underscored enough. Even if the value is self-evident, a business case should still be completed and for the following reasons.

- Secure initial and future funding
- Secure business alignment
- Secure the alignment/realignment of resources
- Demonstrate value and purpose for all program participants
- Serve as a benchmark for which to measure program performance
- Provide insurance against perpetual corporate reorganization

A solid business case has a long lasting influence on executive management and others associated with the program. Some may argue the point but from my perspective this is the very foundation of the entire data governance program. How well the business case is received will determine the short and long term success of the program.

Determine What Is Important

It may all seem important and interconnected; and it is, however there comes a point when you have to focus on those things that matter most. While every organization has their own set of challenges and opportunities, it is imperative that businesses set clear priorities and organize them in a way that are central to solving the majority of their business problems. These priorities should be further divided up between short, mid, and long term objectives with the short term dealing with the 20 percent of activities that drive 80 percent of the business value (80/20 rule).

Take for example an initiative where an organization is attempting to create a 360-degree view of their B2C or B2B business or both. This can be accomplished in a number of ways using technologies and solutions developed for MDM, BI, CRM, EDW, and more. Each of these solutions has a few things in common that are foundational to the success of the project.

- Data integration
- Data quality
- Business process
- Technology
- Data stewardship

If an organization can effectively govern these aspects of the data and information ecosystem they will certainly optimize their results. In other words, business is far more likely to achieve their goals and at a much faster pace. This is not to say there are not other important facets to this equation; however, being able to apply data governance to these alone will have the greatest initial impact on an initiative of this nature.

Create a Concept Definition

Before an organization jumps into the corporate limelight with this thing called data governance, it is reasonable and sensible to develop a concept definition first. Essentially this is about having stakeholders create a high level plan that outlines key aspects of the program and how it will become operational within the business. This exercise should include at minimum:

- Scope definition and prioritization
- Proposed organizational structure
- Lines of authority
- Roles and responsibilities
- Initial and long range scope
- Resource requirements
- Integration into existing and complimentary committees, task forces, and initiatives
- Time commitments of "drafted" or "volunteer" participants
- Performance measurement

The concept should be at a high level but still furnish enough detail to satisfy inevitable questions around proposed changes in operational infrastructure and the time commitments of those involved, especially time sensitive business leaders and executives.

Formally Socialize the Concept and Business Case

Once the business case and concept definition are completed, an organization should consider a formal plan for socializing the concept and the value behind it to executive management, business leaders, and other influential associates. This is a prelude to the formal process of getting the program approved and benefits stakeholder efforts in a number of ways.

- Educates people on the program and the value it brings to the business
- Serves as a reliable feedback mechanism to validate ideas and allows for making modifications and improvements to the concepts prior to formal program approval
- Secures support for the program before the program is ever launched

Having a formal plan to socialize program concepts and value is a critical step given that this discipline involves cross-functional alignment and a non-traditional centralized funding model. Getting people and groups comfortable with the idea ahead of time can make the actual approval process go much easier. Furthermore, it has a long lasting effect. People will be more apt to actively participate since they are aware of the program, the value behind it, and the effort stakeholders made to get them involved early in the process.

Develop and Implement

Once the program has been approved there are a number of activities that will begin to fall into place, most of which I do not cover in this book or this chapter. Remember the title of this book and chapter? Details for implementation of data governance are for another place and time, perhaps another manuscript. However, the following topics and activities will be very important to a successful implementation of data governance.

- Build out and refine the program based on concept definition
- Data governance charter
- Inventory of data, sources, and systems
- Education and training
- Performance metrics
- Meeting management
- Technical implementations
- Data standards
- Time management of business leader participants
- Work flow management
- Integration of complementary groups or committees
- Business alignment
- Monitoring and reporting

- Roles and
  responsibilities
- Data stewardship
- Data architecture
- Business process

- Business rules
- Project planning

The one thing I will say about implementation is that it requires a different focus and skill set to implement governance than it does to develop and oversee the program. For example, a lead stakeholder, mentor, or advisor role should have a good grasp on the business, industry, and technologies. They also should have the aptitude to effectively build a program and alliances at the executive ranks and across lines of business. The implementation role is more tactical with skills honed to lead operational meetings, deal with data centric issues, educate, train, and problem solve the tactical aspects of business process.

While there is certainly overlap, not everyone can effectively fill both roles so it is important to consider a strategy that takes into consideration both requirements. I've seen many instances where someone that is very good at implementation is put in charge of the program and they end up like a fish out of water. I've also seen the reverse where someone with strong program development skills fails at the implementation.

This is equally true when utilizing consulting services to perform the work. There are many quality practitioners that understand the implementation side of the business but struggle with program development or vice versa. This may mean using more than one individual or group to fulfill both roles. The concept applies whether you plan to fulfill these functions internally, externally, or a mixture of both. However, this is actually not a bad strategy either since it also interjects more focus, skills, and points of view into the program, which certainly strengthens overall outcomes.

Methodology

A well thought out, high level methodology can provide exceptional value to any program that is just getting started. It will help keep an organization focused on the right things at the right time, minimize risk, accentuate opportunities, and serve as a guide for filling in project plan details. Methodologies are only as good as the paper they are written on and there are plenty of them circulating around the industry. Whichever one you choose, make sure many of the best practices recommended here are built into the approach and associated program plan details.

Chapter Summary

There is no perfect way to get started with data governance but there are certainly a few best practices that the industry and yours truly have learned from the school of hard knocks. However you choose to get started, keep in mind the following best practices.

- Get help where help is needed, and if you are like most organizations you will need help.

- Take the time to identify and quantify the magnitude of the challenge and opportunities.

- Invest the time to develop a strong business case in order to demonstrate the value.

- Prioritize by identifying what provides the most value given your requirements.

- Formally create a conceptual program before going public with it.

- Develop a formal plan for socializing the concept and value prior to budget approval.

- Consider the different skill requirements needed to build a program verses implement it.

Chances are good that if companies, agencies, and institutions start off strong by following this approach everything else will fall into place. Concentrate on building a solid foundation up front!

Chapter 13

You Know You Have a Problem When

For those that have spent any amount of time in the data quality, governance, and management space, you are all too familiar with the pitfalls and consequences that go with the territory. Especially those glitches that cloud an organization's judgment, derail their approach, and ultimately jeopardize success for data and information management initiatives. This chapter attempts to capture the essence of these wayward practices. More importantly, it aims to keep you and your organization from becoming another statistic.

"You know you have a problem when ..."

1) *You have a MDM, CRM, BI, EDW, 360-degree view or other data sensitive project on the horizon and no provisions have been made for data governance.* You have two choices. Either be prepared to join the long list of organizations that fail to achieve their expectations, or begin putting things in motion to implement a data governance program that can be leveraged in the immediate project as well as for additional projects going forward.

2) *Someone in your organization suggests that technology is the answer to the majority of your data governance problems.* Nice thought, and yes, technology does play a very important role. However, data governance is composed of 80 percent business process and 20 percent technology.

3) *Somebody suggests that data governance is going to solve all your data and information management problems.* Think again. Data governance is a great vehicle for getting your arms around the issues and managing a situation but it does not solve all the problems. In fact, some data problems will be so complex it will be cost prohibitive to fix them; however, governance is certainly the best mechanism for managing the situation.

4) *People in your organization are using the terms data quality and data governance interchangeably to the extent that you are not sure whether they are one in the same, or if they are different concepts.* Take a step back and have someone explain the differences and similarities between the two. A basic 101 approach can go a long way in educating the masses and avoiding conflicts, confusion, and bad decisions down the road.

5) *A person or group notes that while data quality is important, it is not included in the project and that the company will come back and address data quality later.* This is a typical cover for "we did not plan appropriately" for the project. If the funds are not available then someone was not planning or did not think it was important. Organizations that say they will address quality later seldom do. Those that do follow through find the time and expense of fixing data after the fact to be much more costly.

6) *The IT folks do not actively and continuously engage the business or vice versa for any data intensive project.* This is a telltale sign of bigger problems below the surface.

7) *There is one person in the organization that DOMINATES the data quality and data governance discussions, or you are developing your data quality and data governance strategies through the eyes and ears of a*

single person. This is never a good situation, even if these are talented people. These disciplines have too many cross-functional requirements for a single person to master. Every voice needs to be heard!

8) *Someone in your organization says that their data is in "pretty good" shape and there is no reason to conduct a data audit or assessment to determine the quality of the information.* History has proven consistently that it is normally just the opposite and data is worse than expected. People commonly push back on having others look at their data in fear of losing control and/or exposing problems that may reflect negatively on a department or individual.

9) *Your IT or business team is conducting a business value assessment in order to build a business case for data governance.* Organically grown business cases almost always lack the experience required to develop a compelling purpose. In addition, people conducting the exercise are seldom in a position to cross lines of business to collect the information they need. Furthermore, many business cases are project rather than program focused, which can significantly erode the overall value of the discipline. Organizations should consider involving a qualified third party for this exercise.

10) *The sales organization insists on processing transactions with no regard to how data and information is captured*

and leveraged to drive downstream marketing, upsell, and cross-sell opportunities. This is an old, invalid argument. It is time to take a more holistic view of your business. This can be accomplished in a way that respects the sales process but also takes into consideration future revenue streams.

11) *Someone tells you that once data is cleansed and standardized, it has become fit for business purpose.* Not necessarily. Data also must be timely. The best data in the world is useless if it is not available at the right time and for the right reasons. Data also degrades over time after it has been cleansed. For example, names change as people get married and divorced, addresses change as postal codes split, street names change, and phone numbers and e-mail addresses become moving targets over time. This means quality strategies must be governed across the continuum of the data life cycle.

12) *Some in your organization use the excuse that your data management culture is project versus program based and that is just the way it is.* While this will not change overnight, it should not be an excuse for business as usual. Data governance is a good place to start with instilling an enterprise program mindset.

13) *Your IT lead informs you that they fully understand the business requirements and how the business consumes*

company data. Don't bet on it. Assume the opposite. Not to discredit anyone but this is seldom the case. People in IT often understand the very high-level requirements but rarely at the level necessary to optimize outcomes and success. You will want to hear feedback from both the business and IT on this subject.

14) *Your data governance group operates independent of the data quality group and/or you have a corporate data governance group and several independent grassroots data governance initiatives.* I have observed some interesting arrangements in my time but this structure simply does not work nor does it make sense. I am aware of a few companies like this that hit the speaking circuit to tout their success at conferences. When you peel back the onion, you realize they are actually quite dysfunctional because of the way they have segregated the management of their data and information assets.

15) *A vendor tells you "they do data governance."* Huh? What does that mean? Many vendors claim to offer data governance when in fact they are selling the same products and services they always have. Others are making inroads to better support various aspects of this practice, but none do everything this discipline requires and certainly not by automating everything in the process. Remember, 80 percent of this practice is about

business process. The other 20 percent is a collection of specialized technologies.

16) *An associate recommends a grassroots approach where data governance is built into an important project. Once successful, the company can leverage this success in other areas of the organization.* I have always enjoyed being a part of a grassroots effort primarily because they are built on people with a passion to solve the problem and they seldom require much investment. Who can argue with that? The problem with grassroots efforts is that at some point the lawn mower comes by and stunts their growth. The data governance industry is saturated with stories of good intentions that never achieved expectations. In most situations, programs have fleeting success before they go away entirely or remain buried in a single project. The grassroots approach is also a clear indication that the company is not serious about solving their data and information asset problems, or certainly not as serious as they need to be. Is it possible to be successful with grassroots? Yes, is it probable? No.

17) *A colleague notes that you are trying to "boil the ocean" with this top down data governance approach.* The top down approach establishes the discipline as a certified program that can be leveraged across all projects. This is not boiling the ocean. How you choose to scale the program will determine

whether you are perceived as trying to do too much at one time. If you build the discipline out one project at a time or in manageable increments you will be in good shape and should never be accused of boiling anything except age old practices that need to go away.

18) *Someone in your organization suggests that since the business value for data governance is self-evident that you should bypass the process of building a business case.* The problem with this approach is that while the value may be self-evident to a few people today, it probably will not be tomorrow when new players enter the picture. In addition to securing funding, the business case can be used to measure program performance, educate all participants on the purpose of the program, and repel the potential destructive forces of corporate reorganization.

19) *People in the organization are apprehensive to pursue a data governance program because they have already been down that path and executive management shot down their idea and business plan.* I have seen a number of organizations that are in real need of data governance but their first pass with gaining executive buy-in did not go well. The history behind these situations normally involves an initial business case and approach that was full of holes, so naturally it was not adopted by upper management. Don't let past failures stop progress.

Get help, shore up your approach and business case and get moving forward.

20) *Executive leadership is frequently too focused on short term goals to act on long term infrastructure opportunities such as data governance. This can be attributed to job incentives, personal career growth, adversity to perceived risk, and budgets among other things.* If this characterizes your position as an executive then consider changing things up. Otherwise, do not expect individuals in your organization to fix the problems.

"You know you have a solution when ... "

You attend that first data governance leadership team meeting and you hear the dynamic, cross-functional discussions and discoveries evolve, and strategies emerge. From these early meetings come action items that change the way your organization manages, protects, and optimizes its data and information assets.

Chapter Summary

Culture, age old practices, false perceptions, and politics can stop a data governance initiative in its tracks or certainly limit its success. Understanding how to recognize and respond to these hazards is vital to the health of any data governance program.

Conclusion

Data governance can be a complicated maze of strategic and tactical data management activities and business processes whose interdependencies and overall value are seldom clear to an organization. Companies, agencies, and institutions that take the time to understand and holistically act on their data and information assets will benefit in a number of ways that reflect favorably in the bottom line of the business.

This unique discipline is much more than what people see or hear when the term data governance is used. Yes, it is about data, business process, and technology but more importantly it is about formal oversight of the organization's data and information assets. By implementing a recognized infrastructure to administer these assets, it unleashes opportunities and value that cannot be achieved in a business-as-usual environment.

The business value generated by this discipline comes in a variety of forms that collectively, not individually or in a single project alone, optimize project successes and overall business performance. Applying this discipline holistically is the key to high performance, whether this pertains to the enterprise or across the full data and information asset life cycle.

Like any organization, the structure of a data governance program can come in a variety of shapes, sizes, and forms. The important thing is not so much about who reports to whom and how it is organized, but whether it satisfies the fundamental requirements for successful data governance architecture.

Technology plays an important role in automating and implementing data policy. Understanding which technologies are needed and evaluating their core capabilities is an important process for any organization. A well thought out technology direction for data governance is mission critical.

Finally, seriously evaluate the in-house skills and availability of those resources against the requirements for planning and launching a program of this nature. If you are like most organizations, you will probably require some level of assistance from qualified third parties to augment existing skills and resources. Insurance and insight in the right places at the right time is invaluable.

CONCLUSION

As an executive or business leader, you have the opportunity to make constructive changes that will have a profound and long lasting effect on your business, which cannot be accomplished in a grassroots or project based scenario. Don't wait until the next economic downturn to look at ways to cut costs and optimize business performance. The time is now. Data governance, ah...ENTERPRISE INFORMATION ASSET MANAGEMENT is one of the few remaining frontiers for businesses to reduce costs, improve revenues, mitigate risk, and advance business performance.

Embrace the opportunity and good luck in your endeavors!

Glossary

---

360 Degree View – This concept is associated with an organization's attempt to integrate data and information from multiple systems in order to create a holistic view of its customers, partners, and other data domains within their business. The idea is to have a single integrated system and application that users can easily access and that provides all the information they need about their customer, partners, and more.

B2B – Stands for business to business where one organization is transacting business with another company or agency.

B2C – Stands for business to consumer where a business is transacting business with individual customers.

BI – see Business Intelligence.

Big Data – There are various industry definitions floating around, but essentially this represents extremely large and complex data environments that can be so huge and intricate that organizations cannot leverage traditional technologies, applications, and processes to access and manage the data.

BPM – see Business Process Management.

The Business – Refers to people, groups, and functions within the organization with core responsibilities that are business centric versus technical in nature, and for which they have an effect on data outcomes from either a strategic, operational, and/or tactical perspective.

Business Intelligence (BI) – This is the discipline of searching, assembling, analyzing, predicting, reporting, and presenting information for business purposes. It is frequently associated with the technologies that drive business intelligence activities.

Business Intelligence (BI) Governance – Represents the discipline that oversees the standards, principles, practices, and decision making necessary to produce optimal results for business intelligence initiatives.

Business Process Management (BPM) – This is the practice of aligning various business activities in order to drive process improvement and overall efficiencies for the business.

Business Rules – Refers to business logic and constraints that need to be followed to achieve the desired data and information outcomes. Business rules should be developed by the business and implemented within technologies by IT.

Business Transformation – This is normally a corporate initiative that is intended to align business activities more closely with business strategy.

CDI – see Customer Data Integration.

Center of Excellence (CoE) – The CoE is a competency center where specialized skills and resources are centralized for the purpose of leveraging unique capabilities across the enterprise rather than restrict their involvement to a single project or business unit.

CFO – Chief Financial Officer. Also see CxO.

CIO – Chief Information Officer. Also see CxO.

Cloud Computing – Often referred to as "The Cloud." This is where computer services such as data, software, and hardware are hosted by an external provider and where the services are accessed via a computer network through the Internet. Users do not need to install any software on their computer and normally only need a web browser to access the services.

CMO – Chief Marketing Officer. Also see CxO.

CoE – see Center of Excellence.

COO – Chief Operations Officer. Also see CxO.

CRM – see Customer Relationship Management.

Cross-Sell – The process of selling additional products and services to existing customers.

Customer Data Integration (CDI) – This represents the process of linking common customer data across disparate systems for the purpose of creating and maintaining an accurate and complete record of the customer.

Customer Relationship Management (CRM) – Normally associated with the technologies used to organize and automate business processes for managing company prospects, customers, sales operations, marketing, and customer service activities.

CxO – This is a catch all term that refers to "C" level positions such as the Chief Financial Officer (CFO), Chief Information Officer (CIO), Chief Operations Officer (COO), Chief Marketing Officer (CMO) or other high level business executives and decision makers.

Data Governance (DG) – This is the discipline of administering data and information assets across an organization through formal oversight of the people, processes, technologies, and lines of business that influence data and informational outcomes to drive business performance.

Data Life Cycle – This essentially represents the entire data flow of a data domain such as customer or product and represents everywhere the data is entered, moved, stored, modified, analyzed, published, and consumed across the enterprise. It can also include integrated data sources that augment the data domain itself.

Data Management – The discipline of managing data, normally at a tactical level, as it pertains to architecture, modeling, metadata, security, data quality, and more.

Data Mart – A data mart is a subset of an organized data warehouse and is normally leveraged for a specific analytical business purpose within the company.

Data Model – A data model represents how structured data is formatted, referenced, accessed, and stored within databases and information systems.

Data Modeling – The methods and processes followed for developing and maintaining a data model.

Data Quality (DQ) – Refers to the value data has when measured against its ability to meet the desired business purpose (fit for purpose). Such benchmarks commonly take into account correctness, completeness, timeliness, relevance, and accuracy. From a technical perspective it is generally associated with the systems that automate data profiling, parsing, cleansing, standardization, linking, and enrichment.

Data Standards – Represents the harmonization of data content, definitions and formats within and across data sources.

Data Steward – General term that refers to anyone that has a guardianship role and responsibility for the company data at either a business and/or technical level. It is commonly associated with individuals that have physical and/or logical control over the data and are in a position to identify, recommend, and/or make changes to the data itself. Data analysts, subject matter experts, database administrators, and data architects are often categorized as data stewards.

Data Stewardship – This is the practice of coordinating the activities of data stewards across the company and typically involves assigning roles and responsibilities, data ownership, monitoring, measuring, and reporting on data quality and other metrics.

Data Warehouse (DW) – A data repository designed to facilitate information from multiple heterogeneous sources for specific business reporting and analytics.

DG – see Data Governance.

DQ – see Data Quality.

DW – see Data Warehouse.

ECM – see Enterprise Content Management.

EDW – see Enterprise Data Warehouse.

EIAM – see Enterprise Information Asset Management.

EMPI – see Enterprise Master Patient Index.

Enterprise Content Management (ECM) – This is the practice of formally managing an organization's digital and paper documents and other mostly unstructured information. Also known as Content Management (CM).

Enterprise Data Warehouse (EDW) – A centralized data warehouse that is designed to service the entire enterprise. Also see Data Warehouse.

Enterprise Information Asset Management (EIAM) – The author's preferred term to replace the expression of data governance. See Data Governance.

Enterprise Information Management (EIM) – Definition varies, but is frequently associated with the combined practices of data integration, data quality, and data governance with overlap into business intelligence and content management.

Enterprise Master Patient Index (EMPI) – Represents a holistic or global patient index that is created from the Master Patient Index of various healthcare related organizations. Also see Master Patient Index.

Enterprise Resource Planning (ERP) – Represents core business applications that comprehensively manage the company business. ERP systems are designed to manage a number of activities associated with manufacturing, finance, accounting, sales, materials management, distribution, services, customer relationships, and more.

Enterprise Risk Management (ERM) – The practice and process of managing and mitigating organization risk. Very prominent in the financial services industry with emphasis on fraud detection, solvency, and regulatory compliance.

ERP – see Enterprise Resource Planning.

ETL – see Extract, Transform, and Load.

Extract, Transform, and Load (ETL) – This is the process of moving data from one data source into another and is most commonly associated with moving data into a data warehouse. It involves extracting the data from the source system, applying a number of rules (transform) that can join, aggregate, validate, transpose, and even cleanse data before it is loaded it into the target database.

Health Insurance Portability and Accounting Act (HIPAA) – United States law governing a number of things within the healthcare system to include protecting workers and families when they change or lose their jobs, invoking standards for national electronic healthcare transactions, reducing fraud, creating single identifiers for employers, providers, and insurance plans.

HIPAA – see Health Insurance Portability and Accounting Act.

IAM – see Information Asset Management.

IM – see Information Management.

Information Asset Management (IAM) – The author's preferred term to replace the expression of data governance. See Enterprise Information Asset Management.

Information Management (IM) – The organization, dissemination, and maintenance of largely unstructured information across the organization. It has since begun to overlap with data management and data governance.

Information Quality (IQ) – The term is used synonymously with data quality though in some cases it may specifically refer to content information. See Data Quality.

Information Technology (IT) – For the purpose of this book it refers to the authority that manages data centric technologies, applications, and information systems within the organization.

IQ – see Information Quality.

IT – see Information Technology.

IT Governance – This is a high level corporate practice for aligning Information Technology strategies with business strategy.

KPI – Key Performance Indicators.

LOB – Line of business.

M&A – see Merger and Acquisition.

Master Data Management (MDM) – Refers primarily to the discipline of managing mission-critical data elements that lead to the identification and management of common relationships, transactions, and events across multiple disparate systems. The information is synchronized, sometimes within a single database, to create a single or holistic view of the business for the designated business purpose.

Master Patient Index (MPI) – Represents the indexing mechanism for synchronizing patient information within a healthcare system. The purpose of which is to easily link a patient to their medical history, doctors, procedures, medications, billings, and more. Also see Enterprise Master Patient Index.

MDM – see Master Data Management.

Merger and Acquisition (M&A) – For the purpose of this book merger and acquisition pertains to the policies, procedures, and practices that are followed whenever data is brought into the parent organization from outside sources. This can happen when companies purchase and merge with other companies or when businesses acquire third party data.

Metadata Management – Metadata is a vague term that assumes different meanings. It normally refers to "data about data" or "data about data structures". Metadata management is the practice of storing, organizing, and managing information about information. For example, metadata for reports may include the definition of customers included in the report (region, status, etc.), business owner for the report, systems that the data is aggregated from, historical data to be used, calculations to be made, date created, date modified, users of the report, and other critical information necessary to effectively maintain the report.

MPI – see Master Patient Index.

O2C – see Order-to-Cash.

Occupational Safety and Health Administration (OSHA) – This is a United States government agency that oversees and administers safety and health regulations across the country.

OCR – see Optical Character Recognition or Office of Civil Rights.

ODS – see Operational Data Store.

OFAC – see Office of Foreign Assets Control.

Office of Civil Rights (OCR) – A division within the United States government's Health and Human Services department which oversees various HIPPA compliance activities.

Office of Foreign Assets Control (OFAC) – A department within the United States government tasked with monitoring and publishing lists of terrorist and foreign nationals that United States companies are prohibited from conducting business with.

Operational Data Store (ODS) – This is a database that is used to integrate data from multiple systems by taking operational data, performing further processes on the data, and then pushing the results out to both the operational systems and the data warehouse for reporting.

Optical Character Recognition (OCR) – The electronic translation of printed text to electronic format files that can then be used to store, search, edit, print, and display the document in electronic format.

Order-to-Cash (O2C or OTC) – Sometimes referred to as quote-to-cash this represents the end-to-end process of a business transaction and covers all the activities required to initiate an order through to receiving payment for it. It commonly includes activities such as order creation, fulfillment, shipping, purchasing, restocking, invoicing, payment, and more.

OSHA – see Occupational Safety and Health Administration.

OTC – see Order-to-Cash.

PCI – Payment Card Industry.

Personal Information Management (PIM) – The formal practice of studying and analyzing people and how they interact in the work place with the information they need to complete various tasks. One of the goals of this discipline is to improve operational efficiencies by having the right information, at the right time, and for the right reason.

PIM – see Personal Information Management.

Point of Sale (POS) – Sometimes referred to as the point of purchase (POP) and can represent a physical location such as a store, an internet site, a ticket counter, or even a check out terminal within a store.

POS – see Point of Sale.

Reference Data – Refers to information that describes the physical, logical, or virtual properties and characteristics of an object. Examples include customers, patients, products, partners, facilities, and assets. In many respects it is the opposite of transaction data that describes events.

Return on Investment (ROI) – Measuring stick for determining the value of an investment in terms of the time it takes to recoup the initial outlay of capital.

Records Management (RM) – Represents the practice of managing the full life cycle of an organization's records including retention, storage, retrieval, and disposal. This practice is commonly applied in healthcare as it related to a patient's medical records.

RM – see Records Management.

ROI – see Return on Investment.

SaaS – see Software as a Service.

Search – Pertains to technologies that can seek, find, and present information across a collection of structured and unstructured data and information sources within an organization.

SDN – see Specialty Designated Nationals List.

SME – see Subject Matter Expert.

Software as a Service (SaaS) – This refers to software and related data normally hosted by a third party and accessed via the Internet. Also see Cloud Computing.

Specialty Designated Nationals List (SDN or OFAC List) – A list published by OFAC of organizations and individuals with which

United States residents and businesses are prohibited from conducting business. Also see Office of Foreign Assets Control.

Structured Data – Represents data that has predetermined data types and relationships that are understood, such as data stored within databases.

Subject Matter Expert (SME) – Represents an individual who has an exceptional level of knowledge of a certain subject or discipline.

Taxonomy – The practice of classification, normally in a hierarchical fashion. This is a very important aspect to structuring and standardizing data.

Transactional Data – Represents information that describes an event such as a sales order, invoice, payment, purchase, delivery, and more.

Unstructured Data – Represents free form data that has little or no formal data structure. Examples include audio and video files, scanned documents, image files, text documents, e-mail, web pages, word processor documents, PDF, and EXCEL, files.

Upsell – The process of selling customers upgrades and more expensive products and services to increase overall profitability of a sale.

About the Author

For more than 12 years, Jim Orr has had a front row seat in the information management industry as both a leader and as a consultant. Jim's management experience has been cultivated through his leadership positions at Firstlogic, Business Objects, Trilliam Software-Harte Hanks, and Information Builders. His consulting experience comes from working with hundreds of mid-market, enterprise, and global organizations to develop and implement business and technical strategies for their data and information assets. Prior to his information management work he served five years in a leadership capacity in the healthcare technology space. During his career, Jim has worked in nearly every industry vertical and is a frequent guest speaker at a variety of regional, national, and international forums and events.